913-6587

also by Paul Simon

The Songs of Paul Simon
Paul Simon: New Songs

One-Trick Pony

alfred a. Knopf New York 1980

One-Trick Pony

by

Paul Simon

This Is a Borzoi Book
Published by Alfred A. Knopf, Inc.

 Published in the United States by Alfred A. Knopf, Inc., New York, and simultaneously in Canada by Random House of Canada Limited, Toronto. Distributed by Random House, Inc., New York.

Album available on Warner Bros. records and tapes. Matching songbook available from Warner Bros. Publications.

Library of Congress Cataloging in Publication Data
Simon, Paul Frederic [date]
One-trick pony.
I. One-trick pony. [Motion picture]
PN1997.O46 1980 812′.54 80-7636
ISBN 0-394-51381-9
ISBN 0-394-73961-2 (pbk.)

Manufactured in the United States of America
First Edition

Credits

Producer	MICHAEL TANNEN
Co-Producer	MICHAEL HAUSMAN
Director	ROBERT M. YOUNG
Written by	PAUL SIMON
Original Music by	PAUL SIMON
Music Producer	PHIL RAMONE
Editors	EDWARD BEYER
	BARRY MALKIN
	DAVID RAY

Editorial coordinator Eleanor Swan

Photographer Louis Goldman

Cast

Jonah	PAUL SIMON
Marion	BLAIR BROWN
Walter Fox	RIP TORN
Lonnie Fox	JOAN HACKETT
Cal Van Damp	ALLEN GOORWITZ
Modeena Dandridge	MARE WINNINGHAM
Matty Levin	MICHAEL PEARLMAN
Steve Kunelian	LOU REED
Danny Duggin	STEVE GADD
Lee-Andrew Parker	ERIC GALE
John DiBatista	TONY LEVIN
Clarence Franklin	RICHARD TEE
Bernie Wepner	HARRY SHEARER
The B-52's	KATE PIERSON
	FRED SCHNEIDER III
	CINDY WILSON
	RICKY WILSON
The Lovin' Spoonful	JOHN SEBASTIAN
	STEVEN BOONE
	JOE BUTLER
	ZALMAN YANOVSKY
Sam and Dave	SAMUEL D. MOORE
	DAVE PRATER, JR.

Tiny Tim	HIMSELF
Saxophone soloist	DAVID SANBORN
Acappella singers	MICHAEL J. MILLER
	GLENN SCARPELLI
	MERVYN GRIFFITH
	RICHARD DOLAN
Hare Krishna	DANIEL STERN
Blonde girl groupie	LISA CARLSON
Brunette girl groupie	SAMEEN TARIGHATI
Narrator at convention	JOE SMITH
B-52's road manager	STEVE RALBOVSKY
Lawyer	NOEL L. SILVERMAN
Lee Perry	JORDAN CAEL
Cal's girlfriend	SUSAN FORRISTAL
Motor inn clerk	ANN KARELL
Chambermaid	FREDA SCOTT
Receptionists	SKEETER GREENE
	SHARON WATROBA
	CAROL LEVY
	CLAUDIA JO ALLMAND
Bartender	CHARLES TURNER
Backup singers	PATTI AUSTIN
	VIVIAN CHERRY
	ULLANDA McCULLOUGH
Young Jonah	HARPER SIMON
Salesman	GERRY R. BYRNE

Songs

One-Trick Pony

In the night sky the lights of an airplane approach from a distance under the credits. "Late in the Evening" plays over the airplane's approach, which is intercut with the following scenes:

Young Jonah Levin, about seven years old, is playing a toy piano. Then a close-up of him looking out the window.

Four young boys, about thirteen years old, are singing a cappella in a public bathroom. They are dressed in the blackboard jungle, juvenile delinquent look of city kids in the late fifties. They sing the Dion and the Belmonts hit "Teenager in Love" as the camera focuses on thirteen-year-old Jonah Levin.

A bearded, long-haired Jonah Levin appears onstage in front of a giant MCCARTHY FOR PRESIDENT *poster. As he sings his war-protest song "Soft Parachutes," TV monitors pan an enormous crowd.*

Then the body of the airplane becomes visible as it approaches the runway and lands. The luggage ramp is loaded with musical instruments. In a long shot Jonah Levin and his band walk through the airport, carrying instruments, looking tired. As the song concludes and the opening credits fade from the screen, a follower of the Hare Krishna sect comes up to everyone who passes by. He is wearing a cheap suit and a very bad wig meant to conceal the fact that members of this sect shave their heads. He is ignored by each member of the band, now approaching the escalator in single file. He begins to walk with Jonah.

Hare Krishna Excuse me, brother. Can I talk to you for a minute?

Jonah (*Walking, carrying his guitar*) No, thanks, not interested.

Hare Krishna Do you mind if I walk with you? Are you from Cleveland or are you just visiting?

Jonah (*Not looking at him*) I'm really not interested.

Hare Krishna How do you know you're not interested if you don't know what I'm gonna say?

Jonah I know. This is not my first airport.

Jonah comes up the escalator alone. The Hare Krishna climbs the stairs and catches up with him.

Hare Krishna Hey, you're into music, brother? That's wonderful.

Jonah picks up the pace of his walk.

Hare Krishna They're into the Bhagavad-Gita. They even wrote songs about it and everything. Can I give you something?

He offers Jonah a book.

Jonah No.

Hare Krishna C'mon. It's free.

Jonah No thanks. No thanks.

Jonah stops walking and turns to look directly at the Hare Krishna for the first time.

Jonah Look. I've got a lot on my mind right now.

Hare Krishna Krishna has a lot to say about a troubled mind. You should check this out.

Hare Krishna offers Jonah his book again.

Jonah No, thanks.

Hare Krishna You say your mind is troubled. Why don't you check it out? C'mon, brother.

Jonah You know, this is such a minor point. I hate to bring it up, but I *have* a brother.

Hare Krishna We are all brothers.

Jonah No, I mean I have a *real* brother. . . .

Hare Krishna We are all real brothers. That's what I'm telling you.

Jonah No, *this* real brother used to sleep in the other bed in my room.

Hare Krishna (*Handing Jonah a book*) Look, all I'm saying to you is if you want to purify your existence and get into your spiritual self, check this out.

Jonah accepts the book. Hare Krishna grins and pats him on the arm.

Hare Krishna Okay, okay. Hare Krishna.

Jonah nods.

Jonah (*Softly as he walks away*) Okay, okay. Harry Chapin.

* * *

The next shot is of a highway late at night. There is heavy truck traffic. A typical program of pop music and d.j. chatter is being broadcast by radio station WMMS in Cleveland. The camera shifts to a view of the highway as seen from a van—neon signs advertising heroes, pizza, motel rooms. Then a shot of a sign saying BUDGET MOTEL. *The van pulls into the motel parking lot. Jonah and the band enter the motel. At the registration desk, the band members hover alongside or behind Jonah.*

Jonah (*To clerk*) Jonah Levin. Reservation for five rooms.

Clerk (*Looks through reservations*) Here they are, sir (*hands the band registration forms*).

Clarence (*Over Jonah's shoulder as he's signing in*) Excuse me, could I have the room that has the toilet with paper wrapped across the seat?

Clerk All our rooms have toilets like that, sir (*smiles, hands Jonah the key*).

In the next scene, in Jonah's room, a fragment of a song is heard coming from a cassette player. Jonah is in the bathroom, sitting in the tub, shaving. Clarence strolls in.

Clarence Hey, Junior, what time's the first set?

Jonah Clarence. Come right in. Come right in. Taking a bath is usually a private time for me, but I don't mind sharing this moment with you.

Clarence What time's the first set?

Jonah Nine o'clock. But we gotta leave at eight-fifteen.

Clarence looks down vaguely in the area of Jonah's genitals.

Late in the Evening

F
2
B♭
F
F
B♭
F
B
F
F F/G F/G# F/A
A
B♭
The first thing I re- mem- ber I was ly- ing in my
next thing I re- mem- ber I am walk- ing down the
first thing I re- mem- ber When you came in- to my
B♭
3
bed I could-n't have been no more Than one or two
street I'm feel- ing all right I'm with my boys I'm with my troops,
life I said I'm gon- na get that girl No mat- ter what I do
F
B♭
I re- mem- ber there's a ra- di- o
yeah And down a- long the av- e- nue Some
Well I guess I'd been in love be- fore And

B♭
Com- in' from the room next door And my moth- er laughed The way some la-dies
guys were shoot- in' pool And I heard the sound Of A cap- pel- la
once or twice I been on the floor But I nev- er loved no one The way that I
F
C
do
When it's late in the eve- ning
groups, yeah
Sing- ing late in the eve- ning
loved you
And it was late in the eve- ning
F
1. F
2. F
And the mu-sic's seep-ing through
The
Then I
And all the girls out on the stoops, yeah
And all the mu- sic seep-ing through
B
B♭
learned to play some lead gui-tar I was un-der- age in this funk- y bar And I
F
B♭
stepped out-side to smoke my- self a "J"
And when I came back
B♭
to the room Eve- ry- bod- y just seemed to move And I turned my amp up
F
F
C
loud and I be- gan to play
And it was late in the eve- ning
C
F
And I blew that room a- way

C 𝄋𝄋 B♭

F

F

B♭

F

C7

⊕⊕

F

F

𝄋 al ⊕

F/G F/A

⊕ F

F

𝄋𝄋 al ⊕⊕

⊕⊕ Coda "2"

Repeat and fade

Clarence That's it, huh?

Jonah Hey, I am, after all, a Caucasian.

Clarence I understand. And I sympathize.

He leaves.

* * *

The band is performing "One-Trick Pony" in the Agora Ballroom. The players are loose and enjoying themselves. The first shot is of Jonah's guitar reflected in one of the drums. The camera moves to a close-up of Jonah singing and playing his guitar, then swings around to introduce the band: Danny on drums, Clarence on piano, John on bass, and Lee-Andrew on lead guitar. The camera stays with the band until the closing instrumental. Then it moves behind the band to pick up the crowd and the club. The club is a midwestern bar, pine-paneled, with beer signs as the major element of decor. The crowd's response to the music is not enthusiastic; they are talking, drinking, laughing. As the song ends Jonah introduces the band to moderate applause, and as they begin to leave, the audience chants, "Bring on the B-52's." The band exits and the roadies come on to pack up their gear.

Inside the dressing room the B-52's are waiting to go onstage.

First Roadie Sounds like a great crowd. That's it. Everything's ready to go. The Sedalist is up there, right on top.

Second Roadie You got my walkie-talkie up there?

First Roadie Yeah, the walkie-talkie's right by the kids. Time to go. Let's go.

Jonah and the band pass the B-52's on the way back to the dressing room. The B-52's are about twelve years younger than Jonah's band. They dress differently. Borderline New Wave. The two bands nod at each other as they pass. An enormous roar erupts from the audience as the B-52's begin their set. All this is heard from Jonah's vantage point backstage. He walks to the door of the dressing room to watch some of the act from backstage.

The B-52's perform their hit song "Rock Lobster." The performance is intercut with shots of Jonah watching and Jonah's band unwinding in the dressing room. John plays electronic chess. Lee-Andrew fools around with his guitar. Danny tells a story to Clarence, who is laughing and trying to draw Lee-Andrew into the conversation. Jonah is now in the dressing room rolling a joint. A waitress, Modeena, enters carrying a tray.

One-Trick Pony

Am7
2
Am7
2
Am7
He's a one-trick po-ny
One trick is all_that horse can do_
D9
He does_ one trick on-ly_
It's the prin-ci-pal source of his rev-e-nue_
G
D/F#
F
E7sus/B
And when he steps in- to the spot- light, you can feel_ the heat of his heart come
Am7
Am7
ris-ing through_
See how he danc- es
D9
See how he loops from side to side
See how he pranc-es
D9
Am7
G
the way his hooves just seem to glide_
He's just_ a one-
D/F#
F
E7sus/B
Am7
trick pon-y, that's all he is,_ but he turns_ that trick with pride_

C C9 Fma7
He makes it look so eas- y He looks so clean He moves like God's
F#m7(♭5) C/G
im- mac- u- late ma-chine He makes me think a-bout all these
E7/G# Am
ex- tra moves I make, and all this herk-y- jerk- y mo- tion and the bag
C7/B♭ Fma7 B♭9
of tricks it takes to get me through my work-ing day
Am7 Am7 Am7
One-trick pony He's a one-trick pon-y He ei-ther fails
Am7 D9
or he suc-ceeds He gives his tes- ti- mon- y,
Am7
then he re- lax- es in the weeds He's got one
G D/F# F E7sus/B
trick to last a life- time, but that's all a pon- y needs
Am7
that's all he needs
D9 Am7
G D/F#
𝄋 to fade

Modeena (*Rapping on the doorframe*) Excuse me. (*Moving into the room*) Okay. We've got two Heinekens, two Rémy, a sloe-gin fizz, and a Jack Daniel's neat. Club policy is one-third off the menu. Who wants to sign?

Clarence Warner Brothers is paying for it.

Modeena C'mon. You guys aren't with Warner Brothers. I gotta put in a slip with somebody's name on it. So . . . who's it gonna be?

Jonah Doesn't matter. Just leave it here.

A close-up of Jonah looking up and giving the waitress a warm smile.

Jonah I'll sign.

Then a close-up of Modeena.

* * *

Modeena opens the door of her apartment and walks to the kitchen. Jonah follows her in as she pulls on a light cord.

Modeena (*Calling out*) Richie?

Jonah (*Surprised and wary*) Who's Richie?

A dog comes running into her arms.

Modeena He's my dog. I picked him out of a garbage can when he was just a tiny puppy. *Literally*. A garbage can.

Jonah Incredible.

Modeena I know. I was outside the kitchen in the alley behind the club, you know, just grabbing a smoke, when I heard this tiny little whimper and it was him.

Jonah Richie?

Modeena (*Handing the dog to Jonah*) Richie.

Jonah, surprised, holds the dog in his hands while Modeena goes into the bedroom, takes off her coat, brushes her hair.

Jonah then stands in the kitchen, talking to Modeena in the other room.

Jonah I used to have a dog.

Modeena What happened? Did he die?

Modeena returns to the kitchen, goes to the refrigerator, and begins putting the dog's food in a large dog dish. The camera follows Jonah as he walks around her apartment slowly. It is small, with three rooms. The walls are covered with Polaroid photos of rock groups. There is a clutter of books and records, as well as a modest sound system. The conversation continues.

Jonah Oh no. No. He's very much alive. He's my ex-dog. He lives with my ex-wife in my ex-apartment.

Modeena Oh. Do you have any kids?

Jonah I have a son.

Modeena Your ex-son?

Jonah No, he's not in the "ex" group. He'll always be my son.

Modeena Oh. What's his name?

Jonah Matty. You live alone?

Modeena Well, I have a boyfriend if that's what you mean, but we don't live together. I mean, he loves me 'n' all but we don't live together. How long you been divorced?

Jonah Well, I'm actually just separated.

Modeena Separated. So you'll probably try and get back together.

Jonah Where is your boyfriend?

Modeena On the road. He's a roadie.

Jonah He travels a lot?

Modeena A lot. Yeah.

Jonah is in Modeena's bedroom. Her large double bed is covered with a quilt. Jonah turns in the direction of the kitchen.

Jonah What do *you* do when he's gone?

* * *

A medium shot of Jonah and Modeena sitting in the bathtub. Their clothes are on the floor. Modeena is smoking and very involved in a monologue while Jonah listens and plays with the soap.

Modeena . . . so when I got my job waitressing I just quit my other job. It doesn't pay as much as my first job but I get to hear all the rock 'n' roll I want.

Jonah (*Idly playing with the soap*) You really love rock 'n' roll.

Modeena Oh, yeah. It kept me sane when I was a kid.

Jonah Why is that?

Modeena Well, we were always moving around a lot. My dad . . . well, my dad's firm . . . would transfer him to a different city about every year or so. . . .

Jonah What does he do . . . your dad?

Modeena He's an engineer. So I was always having to change houses, change schools, change friends . . . you know how it is. I think that's when I really got into AM radio. 'Cause no matter where I was in the United States, they were always playing the same songs. That was like the thread that ran through my life. AM radio and rock 'n' roll. It kept me sane (*taking soap from Jonah*). Oh, don't use that one. That one's perfumed. Lilac. Where was I? I guess I must have been around thirteen, fourteen . . . anywhere around there. Anywhere around the awkward period. And I decided that I was gonna be a singer. You know, like Janis Joplin. Get up on stage, scream, drink a lot of Southern Comfort. Meet cute guys. Anyway, so I go to my mom and I tell my mom that I'm gonna be a singer. And my mom—I really like my mom—she said, "I never knew you could sing." So I hopped up right there in the living room in front of the TV and I sang the first two verses from "Bobby McGee." Blew her mind.

A close-up of Modeena as she sings the first verses of "Bobby McGee."

* * *

The song "How the Heart Approaches What It Yearns" begins as Jonah leaves Modeena's apartment in the gray Cleveland dawn. He drives the van back to the motel.

* * *

The next shot is of Jonah sitting on the bed in his motel room, in his clothes, talking on the phone. The song continues over the beginning of the conversation, which is barely audible.

Jonah Marion. It's me.

Marion What are you doing up at this hour of the morning?

Jonah Yeah, I know it's early. I had a bad dream and I woke up and I decided to call.

Marion Well, what happened? Is anything wrong?

Jonah Nah. Just a weird dream in a motel room is all.

The song ends with a cut to Marion's apartment. Throughout the conversation, shots of Jonah and Marion are intercut.

Marion is in the kitchen, dressed in a sweater and slacks. Pretty, red-haired, she is about thirty. Matty Levin, six years old, is seated at the kitchen table, eating a bowl of cereal and watching cartoons on television.

Marion Where are you? Matty, will you turn down that TV? I can't hear. It's your father.

Jonah I'm in Cleveland. I just wanted to hear your voice.

Marion What?

How the Heart Approaches What It Yearns

E E E9
1. In the blue___ light Of the Bel- ve-dere Mo- tel___
2. fev- er I dis- tinct- ly hear your voice___ E-
4. phone___ booth In some lo- cal bar and grill___ Re-

A A E E B7
Won-der-ing as the tel- e- vis-ion burns How the heart
merg- ing from a dream, the dream re- turns How the heart
hears- ing what I'll say, my coin re- turns How the heart

1. E 2,3. E E7 Bbm/Gb
ap-proach-es_what it yearns___ In a yearns After the
ap-proach-es_what it I dream we are
ap-proach-es_what it

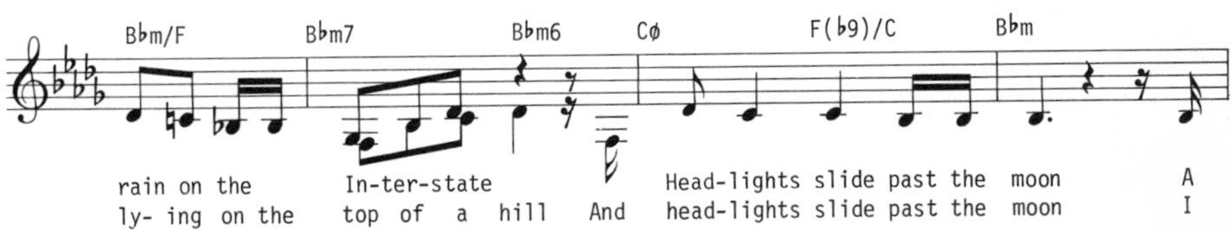
Bbm/F Bbm7 Bbm6 Cø F(b9)/C Bbm
rain on the In-ter-state Head-lights slide past the moon A
ly- ing on the top of a hill And head-lights slide past the moon I

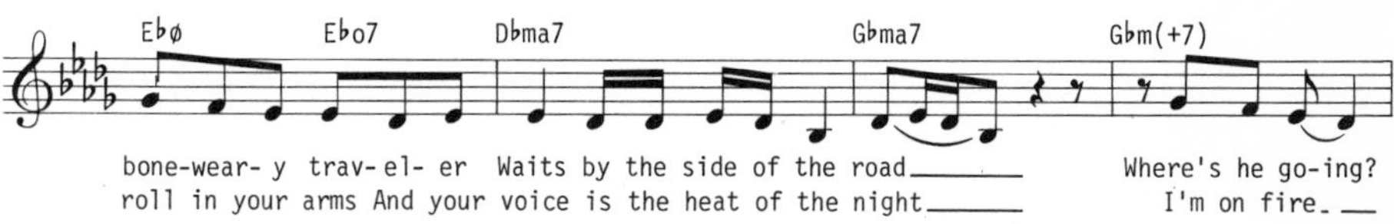
Ebø Ebo7 Dbma7 Gbma7 Gbm(+7)
bone-wear- y trav-el- er Waits by the side of the road___ Where's he go-ing?
roll in your arms And your voice is the heat of the night___ I'm on fire.___

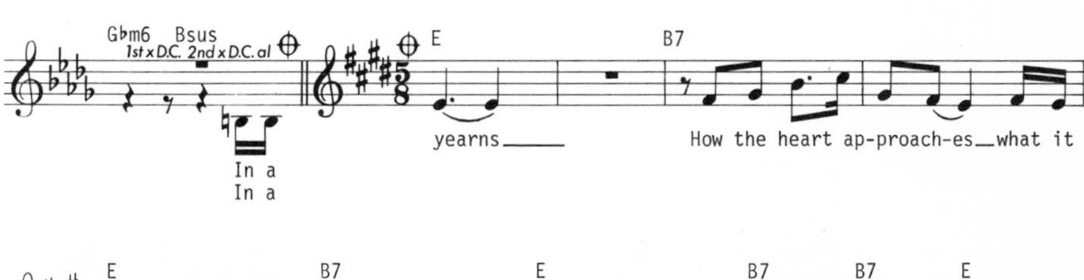
Gbm6 Bsus E B7
1st x D.C. 2nd x D.C. al
In a yearns___ How the heart ap-proach-es_what it
In a

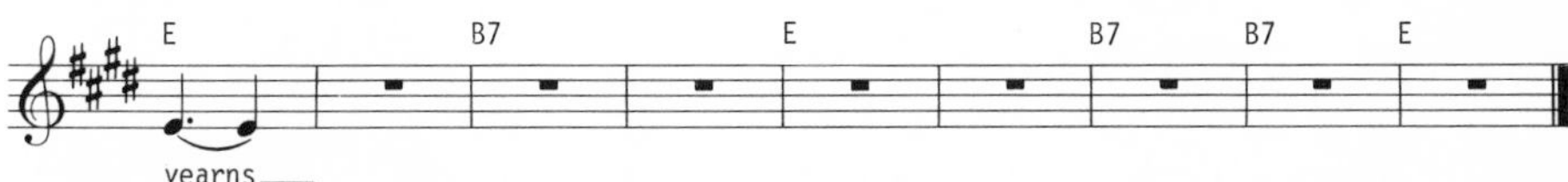
E B7 E B7 B7 E
yearns___

Jonah I said I'm in Cleveland and I just wanted to hear your voice and know that Matty's fine.

Cut to Marion's kitchen.

Marion Christ! A long distance call at six-thirty in the morning. I figure the police are gonna tell me you're dead or something.

Cut to Jonah.

Jonah Not dead. I'm in Cleveland.

Marion Is that it, or is something really wrong?

Jonah Oh, yeah, yeah. Just had a scary dream.

Cut to Marion.

Marion When do you come off the road?

Jonah About ten days.

Marion Then how long will you be in town?

Jonah I'll be in for a little while.

Marion Matty would like to see you. He's a little upset about things.

Cut to Jonah.

Jonah Well, he could stay with me for a couple of days when I get back next weekend after Dayton.

Marion Yeah . . . Jonah, I made an appointment for a meeting with the lawyers. We both have to be there to sign.

Jonah Well, why do we both have to be there?

Marion Well, that's what they said.

Jonah Well, why don't we say that we'll sign it separately?

Marion That's what they said.

Jonah Yeah, well, I don't particularly look forward to having your lawyer and my lawyer . . .

Marion Look, I don't look forward to it either.

Jonah Well, that's why we should call them and say we wanna ...

Marion I don't think we should talk about it right now, okay?

Jonah Okay.

Marion Okay. Well, goodbye.

Jonah Okay. Goodbye.

Marion hangs up, then walks over to Matty and kisses him on the cheek.

Marion Your father said to give you a big kiss. You're gonna sleep over at his new apartment when he comes home.

A shot of Jonah lying on the bed in the motel room.

* * *

In a long shot, Jonah's van is passing through the beautiful midwestern fall countryside. During the following scene, long aerial views of the van passing through the countryside, driving in traffic around cities, continuing along the highway, are intercut with close-ups of the band. Jonah is driving and John is sitting next to him doing a crossword puzzle. Danny and Lee-Andrew are in the middle seat. Clarence is in the back, instruments piled high behind him. At the start of the song "God Bless the Absentee," Danny is reading the Cleveland Plain Dealer. *Turning the pages, he stops at the entertainment section. As Danny begins speaking, Jonah is only half listening and John keeps doing his crossword puzzle. The song continues under the dialogue.*

Danny Okay. Here we go. We got reviewed. All right! "Two bands perform at the Agora."

The band members now perk up. They are interested in the review.

Danny "The Agora presented an evening of diverse musical styles last night when it paired a 'new wave' band, the B-52's, with the veteran Jonah Levin Band. The B-52's are the latest darlings of the anarchic new wave of rock that is sometimes called punk."

Clarence Skip that shit. Let's hear about us.

Danny This is it. "Former regulars on the club circuit, this highly regarded band of the late sixties and early seventies hasn't appeared in Cleveland for some time. Perhaps this accounted for the muted reception that greeted their performance in the early show last night."

Clarence (*In surprised disagreement*) Muted reception? He calls that a muted reception?

Danny "However, Levin's scruffy band of misfits . . ." Well, we can all relate to that. ". . . turned in a more than creditable set. The drummer, whose name I didn't get . . ." Fuckin' great. ". . . was as solid as a metronome. The bassist and piano player were equally competent, if uninspiring."

Clarence Uninspiring! (*He snorts with disgust.*)

Danny "Lead guitarist Lee-Andrew Parker was a real gem, playing some of the most mellifluous solos this reviewer has heard in a long time."

Lee-Andrew What's mellifluous?

Danny I think it's basically about the same as bodacious.

Danny "The band's fifty-minute set consisted of mostly familiar Levin compositions, though he did leave out 'Soft Parachutes,' his anti-war hit of the late sixties. Levin himself seems somewhat less ambitious these days, or maybe we just caught him on an off night. The fire of his earlier work seems to have dimmed somewhat although sparks were still visible at the Agora last night." That's it.

Clarence Well, fuck him.

Danny Yeah, fuck him.

There is a moment's pause.

God Bless the absentee

Clarence Yeah, who gives a shit.

John Who gives a shit.

They all are silent for a while. Finally:

Lee-Andrew Can you read that part about me again?

* * *

It is a sunny day in Washington Square Park. Marion, carrying packages from the supermarket, walks down the street. Jonah is sitting on the stoop.

Marion What are you doing here?

Jonah I used to live in this building. I thought I'd come visit my old room.

Marion I thought you were supposed to be in Dayton.

Jonah I came home early.

Marion How come? Weren't you working?

Jonah and Marion, both carrying packages, enter Marion's apartment. Jonah looks around as he enters the kitchen.

Jonah I remember this.

Jonah goes to a large asparagus fern hanging in the window.

Jonah I see the old fern's doing well.

Marion Yes, the fern is doing well. It's doing very, very well.

Jonah Spray it regularly, do ya?

Marion Spray it every day. Talk to it. Give it lots of encouragement.

Jonah (*Whispering*) You haven't told it about our separation, I hope.

Marion (*Whispering*) Absolutely not. I don't think it would be wise at this time. It's just beginning to sprout new leaves.

Jonah Where's Matty?

Marion It's only two o'clock. He's got his play group on Wednesdays.

Jonah Oh, yeah. I'll bet he'll be surprised to see me.

Marion stops for a minute, looks at Jonah as if to speak, then turns and continues putting groceries away.

Marion My mother came down for a few days last week.

Jonah That's nice. How's ole Florence doin'?

Marion She's fine, I guess. You know, it's the same old story with her. Broad hints about reconciliation, that sort of thing. After two days I am ready to scream. . . . I'd like to talk to you about Matty.

Jonah wanders around the kitchen as Marion talks. He looks in the refrigerator and turns around, feigning indignation.

Jonah No strawberry yogurt?

Marion No. You're the one who likes strawberry yogurt.

Jonah (*Closing the refrigerator*) Boy, you get a little separated and you can just forget it for your strawberry yogurt. What about Matty?

Marion He wants to be a songwriter and play in a band.

Jonah Role-model identification.

Marion I wish you could supply him with some other role to model himself after.

Jonah crosses the kitchen toward Marion and leans on the counter, where she is still sorting groceries.

Jonah I don't see anything wrong with the model he's got now.

Marion It hasn't turned out to be so great for you.

Jonah I don't know. It hasn't been bad.

Marion It's been fifteen years.

Jonah (*Turning and walking away*) Fourteen.

Marion It's the longest adolescence I have ever seen. Well, admit it. In six years you'll be forty years old. Now you've gone directly from adolescence to middle age.

Jonah In six years I'll be forty years old. In sixteen years I'll be fifty years old. In twenty-six years I'll be sixty years old. In a mere sixty-six years I'll be a hundred years old.

Marion A grown man living in a kid's world.

Jonah has picked up a doll and makes its mouth move as if repeating the line:

Jonah A grown man living in a kid's world.

Marion You don't always have to be sarcastic.

Jonah I'm not always sarcastic. Well, I was sarcastic in the late seventies, I admit it . . . seventy-seven, seventy-eight. But really since . . . February seventy-nine, I've hardly been sarcastic.

Marion You see, that's sarcastic.

Jonah Well, what do you expect? "A grown man living in a kid's world"? What do you think I'm doing out there, cashing in my tickets for a ride through the Magic Kingdom? Playing my gigs in the Haunted House?

Marion No. What I mean is, you have wanted to be Elvis Presley since you were thirteen years old. Well, it's not a goal that you're likely to achieve. He didn't do so well with it himself. Isn't it time you gave up the illusion?

Jonah Wait a minute. I know that voice. That's Engleheart about to deliver her "Be a Grownup" speech. Isn't that so, Dr. Engleheart?

Marion I really think you ought to examine your hostility to Dr. Engleheart.

Jonah I have no "hostility" to Dr. Engleheart. I'm just tired of hearing Engleheart's toy phrases come out of your mouth.

Marion They are not toy phrases. She observed, I am merely passing on the observation, that *kids* listen to rock 'n' roll and *kids* play it.

Jonah Well, is she aware that Anna Freud, *Anna Freud,* happens to love rock 'n' roll? She came backstage and sold us some blow after a show in Akron, Ohio. That's where she lives.

Marion (*Smiling*) You want a cup of coffee?

Jonah (*Begins helping Marion with cups*) Yeah, any stimulants will do.

Marion Look, everyone's getting older. I'm not saying it's bad. But, I don't know, rock 'n' roll when you get to a certain age . . . it's kind of . . . it's pathetic.

Jonah (*Angry again, turns to leave the apartment*) Y'know, I gotta go. It's been great, as usual.

Jonah exits into the hallway. Marion goes after him.

Marion What are you afraid of, anyway? That young girls won't like you when you're on the road?

Jonah (*Stops putting on coat*) You know what I'm afraid of? You know what I'm afraid of? I'm afraid of you boring me to tears.

Marion (*Hurt and angry*) Boring you to . . .

Jonah Yeah. You are so fucking boring.

She turns and picks up coffee cups and goes to the sink and begins to wash them. Her back is to Jonah who stands embarrassed and awkward, leaning against the kitchen doorway.

Jonah (*Sighs*) I'm sorry, Mare.

He goes to the sink to help wash the cups and saucers. Their hands touch in the sink.

Jonah (*Gently*) I don't know what you want, Mare. You want me to drive a cab? You want me to give guitar lessons to thirteen-year-old kids? I'm just a player. That's all I know how to do.

Marion I just want . . . I just wanted . . . I wished that when you *were* here, you were *really* here. I mean really with us. Not just sleeping here and talking on the phone or trying to write songs. But here. A family. The road is the road. This was supposed to be home.

Jonah It was home.

Marion (*Tears in her eyes*) Not really.

Johan (*He kisses her tears*) I'm sorry, Mare.

* * *

On the baseball field in Central Park Jonah and Matty are involved in a two-man baseball game. Jonah gives a running commentary from the pitcher's mound while Matty concentrates on the game and responds whenever necessary.

Jonah Great day for baseball here in Yankee Stadium. The New York Yankees take on the Boston Red Sox. On the mound for the Red Sox is their ace and fantastic star Dennis Eckersley. (*As Frank Messer*) I'm Frank Messer. (*As Phil Rizzuto*) And I'm Phil Rizzuto. We'll be broadcasting the game today. We should be ready to begin right now. Eckersley has finished his warm-ups. First batter for the Yankees will be . . .

Matty (*Ready to bat, shouts*) Reggie Jackson!

Jonah Reggie Jackson! Just entering second grade at the Little Red School House in Greenwich Village. Reggie digs in. Look at the concentration on him. Incredible! Here comes a pitch. Swung on and missed. Strike one. And Eckersley is lookin' very sharp today. He's throwin' smoke up there, throwin' smoke.

Camera moves to Matty.

He's knockin' some dirt off his spikes.

Back to Jonah.

And Eckersley looks in, looks around for the pitch. And it's . . . swung on and missed! Good swing. It was a very good swing. It was a miss but it was a very good swing!

The game goes on. Jonah pitching and Matty at bat.

Jonah Looked like he's goin' for the bleachers, didn't it, Phil? Certainly did, Frank. He's almost up to fractions, now, the Reg. Yep. That second-grade class is movin' at a fantastic pace. It's really amazing that a guy can learn fractions, still be here in the last day of the American League pennant race. Well, that's just the kind of kid he is. Eckersley looks in for the sign. And the pitch! Reg swings. It's swung on. That could be outta here! It did travel! And Reg is around first. Around second.

Matty hits the ball. Jonah runs for it as Matty trots around the bases.

This could be a home run! This could be the play at the plate. And here he comes down to third base. Yes, he's safe.

NY

When Matty touches home plate, he raises his arms above his head, fists clenched.

A fantastic play! And Eckersley goes in for the call. They're sayin' he missed the plate. (*To Matty*) Did you hit that plate?

Matty (*Adamantly*) Yes!

Jonah Well, it's a home run for Reg!

Jonah and Matty hug and leave the park.

* * *

As the song "Nobody" begins, Jonah and Matty are on the subway. Both are reading newspapers, struggling to fold them, pointing out things while they talk to each other. Matty is holding a hedgehog mask in his lap.

Jonah and Matty walk back to Marion's apartment. They are talking, laughing, holding hands. They both go inside. They come out of the elevator on Marion's floor. Matty is wearing the mask, which covers his entire head. As they creep around the corner of the hallway Marion is standing in the doorway waiting for Matty. She waves to Jonah as she and Matty go inside and close the door.

* * *

The separation agreement is read over the following while "Nobody" plays in the background.

Voice-over "Agreement of separation made this fourteenth day of November nineteen seventy-nine between Jonah Levin and Marion Levin . . .

Nobody

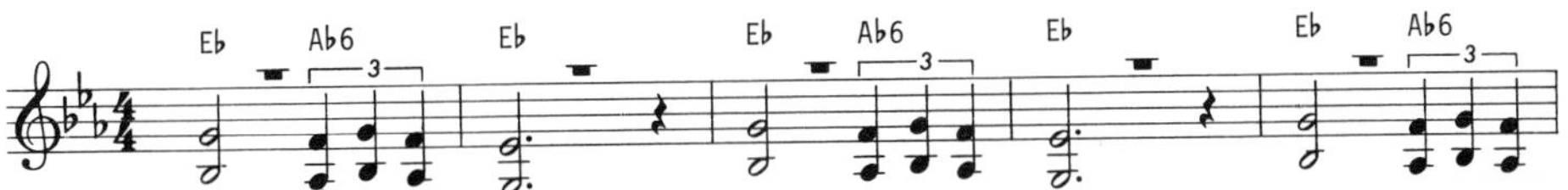

Eb Ab6 Eb Eb Ab6 Eb Eb Ab6

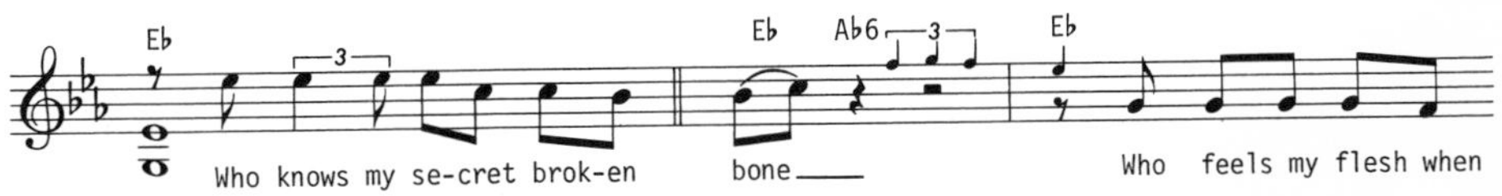

Eb Eb Ab6 Eb
Who knows my se-cret brok-en bone___ Who feels my flesh when

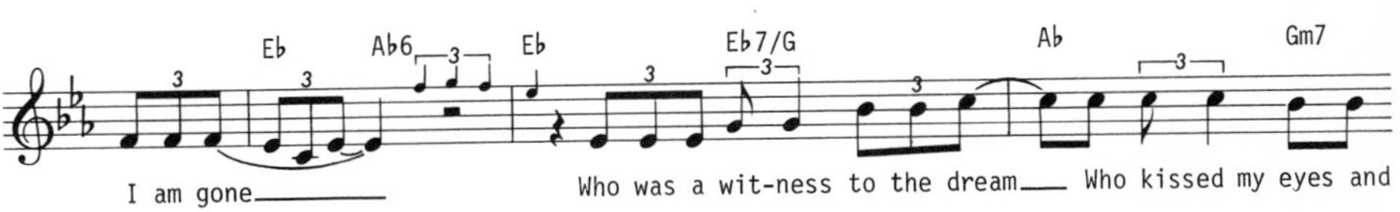

Eb Ab6 Eb Eb7/G Ab Gm7
I am gone_____ Who was a wit-ness to the dream___ Who kissed my eyes and

F9 Ab/Bb Eb Eb
saw the scream___ Ly-ing there___ No-bod- y Who is my rea-son to be-

Eb Ab Eb Eb Ab Eb
gin_____ Who plows_the earth, who_breaks the skin Who took my

Eb7/G Ab Gm7 F7 Ab/Bb
two hands and made them four Who is my heart, who is my door Nobod-

Eb Ab Eb Db9 Cm7 Bb7
y No-bod-y but you, girl No-bod-y but you

Cm7 Eb9 Ab Gb B Db
No-bod-y in this whole wide world No-
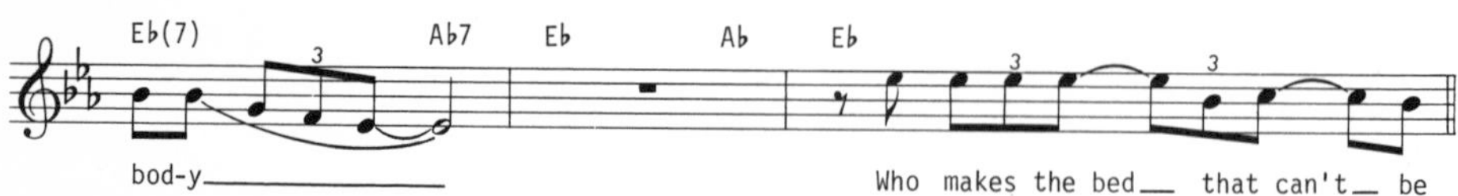
Eb(7) Ab7 Eb Ab Eb
bod-y Who makes the bed that can't be

Eb Ab6 Eb Ab
made Who is my mir-ror, who's my blade

Eb Eb7/G Ab Gm7
When I am ris- ing like a flood Who feels the pound-ing in my blood
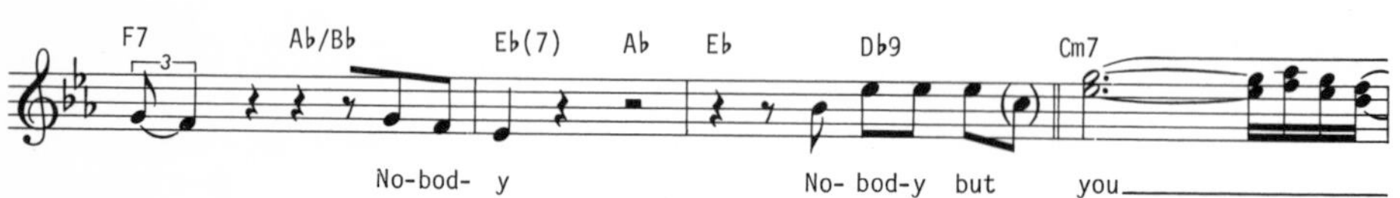
F7 Ab/Bb Eb(7) Ab Eb Db9 Cm7
No-bod- y No- bod-y but you

Bb Cm7 Eb9 Ab Gb
No- bod-y but you, girl No- bod-y in this whole wide

B Gb Cb7 Gb Db Bb/D Eb Ab
world Nobody, girl Nobody

Eb Eb Ab Eb Eb7/G Ab Gm7 Ab/Bb Eb Ab
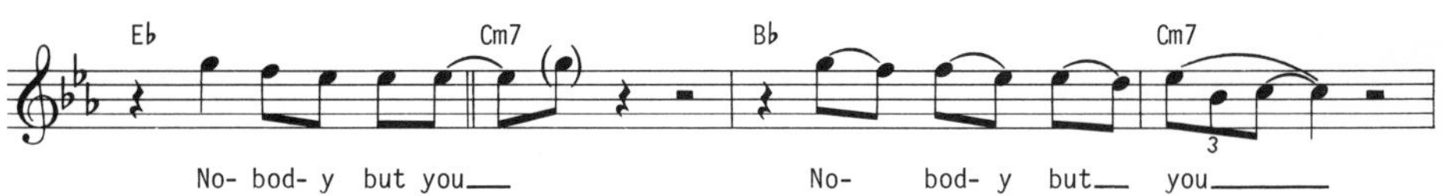
Eb Cm7 Bb Cm7
No- bod- y but you No- bod- y but you

Eb9 Ab Gb Cb Db
No- bod-y in this whole wide world No-bod-
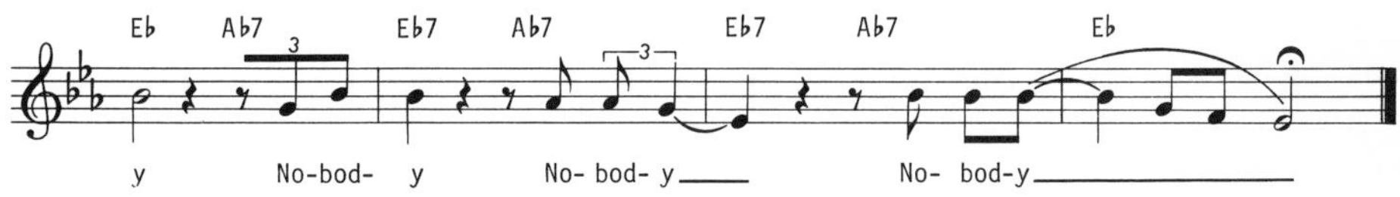
Eb Ab7 Eb7 Ab7 Eb7 Ab7 Eb
y No-bod- y No- bod- y No- bod-y

"The parties herein referred to were married on the twenty-fifth day of December nineteen sixty-nine in New York, New York.

"The parties have one child, Matthew Levin, born August twenty-third, nineteen seventy-three.

"Article One. It shall be lawful for the Wife and Husband to live separate and apart from each other for the rest of their lives, free from interference, authority, or control by the other, as fully as if he or she were single and unmarried. . . ."

A shot of Jonah in a white shirt, hair combed back, tying a tie in the mirror.

A shot of Marion in her bedroom, dressed and brushing her hair in the mirror.

A shot of a subway train moving through a station and a close-up of Jonah in one of the cars.

A shot of a bus moving down a street and a close-up of Marion on the bus. The bus pulls up in front of a glass high-rise office building and Marion gets out, walks through the crowded street.

Jonah also walks through the crowded street.

In the lawyer's office, Marion and Jonah sit at a small conference table facing each other with their lawyers at their sides. The separation agreement is on the table between them. The voice finishes reading the agreement and both sign as the song "Nobody" ends.

Voice-over ". . . in witness whereof the parties hereto have signed this agreement. . . ."

* * *

Jonah is in the kitchen of his apartment. The sink is full of dirty dishes. He throws another knife into the mess and walks into the other room eating an English muffin. The apartment is sparsely furnished, the bed is not made, books, boxes, and guitars line the walls in piles. The telephone answering machine plays back messages throughout this scene.

Clarence's Voice Hello, Junior. We're just sittin' out here waitin' to play some music, so finish up the divorce and get your ass back on the road. Everyone says "hi."

The beep sounds. Jonah crosses from the kitchen into the main room, still listening.

Matty's Voice Dad, Mommy wants to know if this is the weekend I'm staying at your house.

Marion's voice is in the background, as Jonah sits on the bed and starts to softly strum his guitar.

Marion's Voice Tell him to call back.

Matty's Voice Call back . . . Bye.

He hangs up. The beep sounds.

Bernie Wepner Jonah, Bernie Wepner. Listen, Walter Fox is willing to meet you at his apartment and give a good listen to some of your new material. Call Debby for the address. I don't have it right in front of me.

After the machine goes off, Jonah picks up a guitar from the bed, sits down, and starts to play.

* * *

Jonah is in Walter Fox's lavish hotel suite with Walter, Cal Van Damp, and Steve Kunelian. It is a huge room with speakers, a tape deck, and stereo equipment set up. On a table are the remains of a room service meal, trade papers, and a gold cigarette lighter.

Walter (*As Jonah sets up*) I think it is very important for you to make the right record at this time. Not only from a career standpoint but also from a . . . really . . . a whole industry view because you're known as someone who's been around for a while and people feel, perhaps erroneously, that they know you, and don't pay as much attention as they might to something that's new, that's flashy, or not necessarily flashy but new and . . .

Jonah starts the Rhythm Ace.

Walter Cal, I'd like to hear what you think, you know, through the ears of AM radio.

Cal You can have my opinion for what it's worth.

Steve For what it's worth? Cal, you have uncanny AM ears.

Cal Thanks. Twenty years of AM ears. That's what they're calling this profile piece that *Billboard* is doing on me. "Twenty Years of AM Ears." Did I tell you they were doing a profile?

Walter No. Congratulations, Cal. (*To Jonah*) Jonah, I don't mean to rush you, but play what you consider to be your strongest material first.

Jonah Ah, this song is called "Ace in the Hole." It's been going over really well in the clubs we've been playin'. The only thing about it is that we alternate verses. I sing the first verse and then Clarence Franklin, who's our keyboard guy in the band, sings the second verse. So when you hear the second verse you have to sort of imagine that it's another voice

Jonah starts to tune up, begins the opening chords, and starts to sing. At this point Lonnie Fox, about forty to forty-five years old, enters from the bedroom. She is tall, strikingly good-looking. Cal rises.

Walter Cal, this is my wife, Lonnie.

Cal Nice to meet you.

Lonnie How do you do.

Walter And this is Jonah Levin.

Lonnie Hello.

Jonah Hello.

Walter Jonah was playing an exciting new song.

Lonnie (*Holding an unlit cigarette*) I was just looking for some matches.

Cal jumps in with a gold lighter.

Cal Don't go any further

Lonnie Thank you.

Walter Sit down, dear. It's exciting material.

Jonah (*A little uneasy*) This is just a voice and guitar.

Lonnie If you'd rather I left, I'd understand. I won't be offended.

Cal No. Stay, really. Jonah won't mind.

Walter All right, Jonah. Let me hear one of these great new songs.

Jonah I'll take it from the second verse.

Jonah begins to play "Ace in the Hole." He stops and explains what happens when the band plays the song—that Clarence joins him on the vocals. As he plays, Walter toys with his glasses, fixes his hair, rubs his eyes. Cal and Steve listen impassively. Lonnie is visible behind Jonah as he plays. The phone rings as Jonah begins the second verse.

Walter (*To Steve*) Tell whoever it is I'll call back.

Steve comes over and whispers to Walter, and Walter takes the call. The camera pans the room as Walter talks. Jonah, Steve, and Cal all seem to be watching Walter. Lonnie watches Jonah.

Walter (*To Jonah*) I've got to take this call (*picks up the phone, talks to one of his major artists*). Hello, my friend. You've heard the good news, I presume? No? Well, your record is getting major across-the-board acceptance. Listen to this . . . (*He reads from a sheet of paper*) *Record World* "Most Added" list . . . fourteen, first week. And here, listen to this . . . "Feels Like I'm in Love Again" . . . a stone-faced smash. Explosive sales. Twenty to eleven, KFRC . . . Twelve to four on WIXY. KHJ reports great demographic record. Enters at number nine, first week. Are you happy? Good. (*He listens*) The billboard on the Strip is of no value sales-wise. I've told you that. In all honesty it really is a pure ego trip. I must be honest and tell you that. No, no, no. It's not the money. My friend, I will gladly spend the money if you . . . if you want the billboard, you've got it. Are you happy? Well, you should be. Okay. Goodbye. Goodbye. (*To Cal*) Jonah, I'm sorry. Let's hear. What else have you got?

Jonah I could do a ballad. It's called "Long, Long Day."

Jonah plays the tune "Long, Long Day."

Walter It's nice. Please don't misunderstand what I'm about to say. It

just misses. It's pretty, but . . . the Top Forty is getting much more sophisticated. It's very hard with a ballad.

Cal Song's got no hook.

Jonah looks blankly at Cal.

Cal A hook! A hook! Repetition of a catchy phrase. A hook!

Jonah I know what a hook is.

Cal goes to stand in front of the fireplace. A hunting print is visible behind his head.

Cal Look, sixty-five percent of AM programming today is disco. You got no hook you're at an incredible disadvantage in the Top Forty. . . . You know, I'm rotating twelve songs. That's it. You get a new Manilow, a new Donna Summer, a "Feels Like I'm in Love Again," you gotta make room.

Jonah Look, I . . . this is just a voice and guitar. But when I play with my band . . .

Cal (*To Walter*) Well, of course, if you play the big arenas and stadiums you can bust an act like that too. 'Course, a lot of people will tell you it ain't music in those places. It's spectacle. But here's my point, and this is what I said in my profile. . . . Music, spectacle, what's the diff? If it sells records.

Walter That's true.

Cal In fact, I said to the guy at *Billboard,* I said, "I'm a funny kind of guy, but I'll stick my neck out and say that Presley and the Stones are the only act that successfully combined music and spectacle." Maybe Springsteen.

Jonah How about Albert Schweitzer?

Lonnie laughs.

Cal Who's Albert Schweitzer?

Jonah You know, Africa, the organ, disease. Albert Schweitzer, the king of music and spectacle.

Cal What label is he on?

Lonnie can't stop laughing.

Walter Cal, I think Jonah's just kidding you.

Cal Hey. I like a good joke. If it's funny.

* * *

Cut to the band performing "Ace in the Hole" in a club.

* * *

Cut to the van passing through an industrial landscape—through towns and past railroad yards. The back of the van is piled high with instruments. Jonah sits in the middle seat with Danny. John is in back reading. Clarence is driving. The camera moves from one to the other in close-up.

Jonah King Curtis.

Danny Donny Hathaway.

Clarence Otis Redding. The greatest. "Dock of the Bay" was just becoming a hit when he went down in that plane. Man, I just cried.

Lee-Andrew Sam Cooke.

Danny John, you wanna play some "Rock 'n' Roll Deaths"?

John (*Putting down the book he is reading*) Yeah, I'll play.

Danny Put up your twenty bucks.

John (*Antes up twenty dollars*) Jimi Hendrix.

Jonah The late, great Buddy Holly.

Clarence Bobby Darin.

Danny He's not technically rock 'n' roll, you know.

Jonah Yeah, he qualifies. "Splish Splash," "Queen of the Hop."

STAMPEDERS
NEW
WAY

Danny That's early stuff. Later he was strictly Vegas.

Jonah What about that Tim Hardin tune.

John "If I Were a Carpenter"?

Jonah "If I Were a Carpenter."

Danny I don't think that technically qualifies as rock 'n' roll, but let's not quibble. Anyway, now that you mention him—Tim Hardin.

Clarence He ain't dead. You're out.

Danny Bullshit I'm out. He OD'd.

Clarence He did not OD. He's still alive. He lives up in Woodstock.

John Croce.

Jonah Croce's good. We should have two separate categories. For the OD's and the plane crashes.

Danny Nonono. . . . We're playin' for money here. Let's just get the names together.

(*The following dialogue is spoken rapidly.*)

Jonah Okay. Mama Cass. Cass Elliot.

Lee-Andrew Richie Valens

Clarence Van McCoy.

John Lynyrd Skynyrd.

Jonah You only get one point for that. Ah, the fifties rock 'n' roll guy . . . Be-bop-a-lula . . . Gene Vincent.

Clarence The guy from Chicago. Blew his brains out. Terry . . . Terry somethin' or other.

Jonah There must be some English guys who died. We just don't pay attention that much. English dead people . . . English dead. . . .

Long, Long Day

Oh, yeah. Eddie Cochran. He's not English, he died in England.

John Who is it? Eddie Cochran?

Jonah Yeah. "Summertime Blues."

Danny All right. The first drummer with the Average White Band. Robbie . . . Robbie . . .

Jonah Right. Robbie OD'd at Cher's place.

Danny OD'd at Cher's place was his last name?

Jonah No. That's where he . . .

Danny Let me see. Janis Joplin.

John Joplin's good. Elvis.

Jonah Yeah. He's dead.

* * *

Camera begins to pan and we see the band and the audience in the semi-dark in a smoky club decorated with beer signs. We see pinball machines, a pool table, a jukebox.

After the performance that night the band drives through the streets of Ashtabula, smoking grass.

Clarence (*Inhaling deeply on the joint*) Hey, man, when we play the Rising Sun?

Jonah is driving the van. Two groupies have come along.

Danny (*Trying to light a joint*) Please, God, let it light. What'd you say your name was?

Groupie Darlene.

Everyone is laughing and in good spirits.

Danny Did you ever see one of these before? (*Groupie laughs.*)

Clarence figures that chubby little waitress is still waiting for him.

Clarence Man's gotta eat.

* * *

The following visuals are seen as the song "Jonah" is heard as score. There is a party in Jonah's room. Jonah, Danny, and the blonde groupie are sitting on the bed, smoking, drinking, laughing, talking. Clarence is off in another part of the room dancing with the brunette groupie. The scene is covered by a series of vignettes which dissolve into one another, creating a time lapse. Each shot is a slow pan. The song "Jonah" continues as the party goes on. Toward the end the camera shows

Jonah

E♭m11
A♭9/E♭
E♭m11
A♭9/E♭
E♭m
B♭/D
1. Half an hour change your strings and tune
2. No one gives their dreams a-way too light-

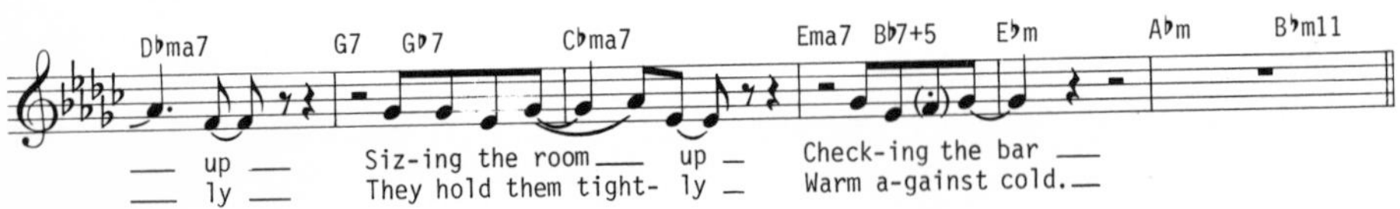

D♭ma7
G7
G♭7
C♭ma7
Ema7
B♭7+5
E♭m
A♭m
B♭m11
up
ly
Siz-ing the room up
They hold them tight- ly
Check-ing the bar
Warm a-gainst cold.

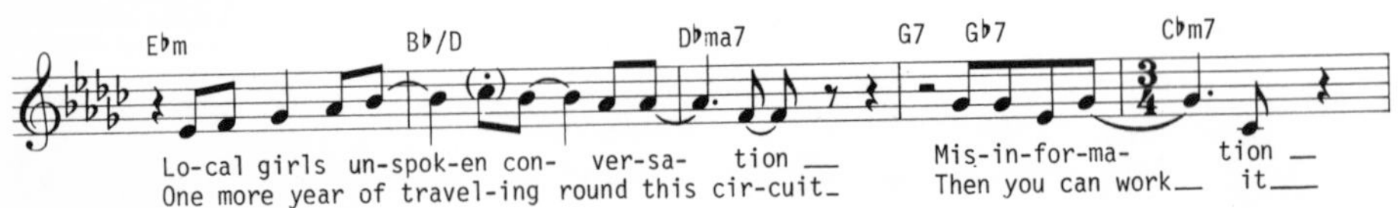

E♭m
B♭/D
D♭ma7
G7
G♭7
C♭m7
Lo-cal girls un-spok-en con- ver-sa- tion
One more year of travel-ing round this cir-cuit
Mis-in-for-ma- tion
Then you can work it

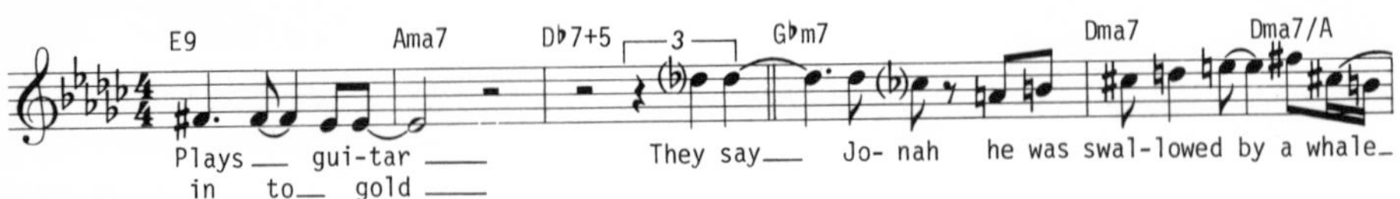

E9
Ama7
D♭7+5
G♭m7
Dma7
Dma7/A
Plays gui-tar
in to gold
They say Jo- nah he was swal-lowed by a whale

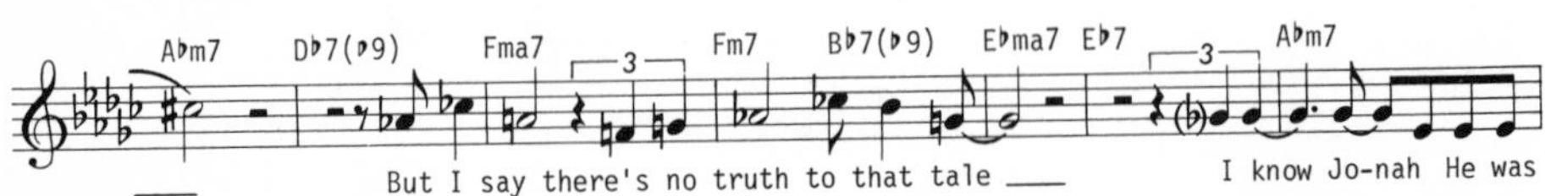

A♭m7
D♭7(♭9)
Fma7
Fm7
B♭7(♭9)
E♭ma7
E♭7
A♭m7
But I say there's no truth to that tale
I know Jo-nah He was

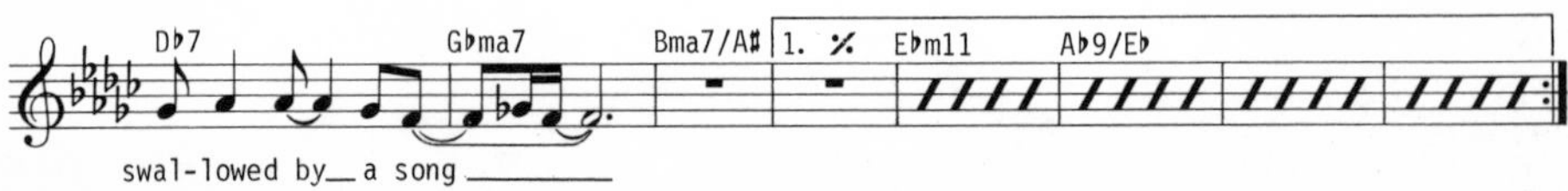

D♭7
G♭ma7
Bma7/A♯
1.
E♭m11
A♭9/E♭
swal-lowed by a song

2.
E♭𝄋
A♭𝄋
Gm7
Gm7/D
Here's to all the boys who came a- long Car-ry-ing soft

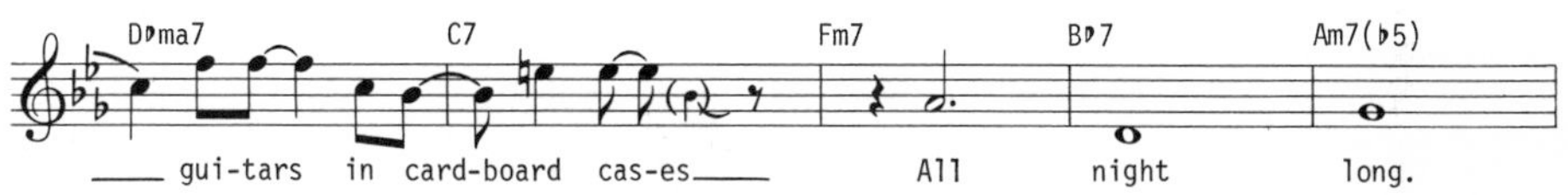
D♭ma7
C7
Fm7
B♭7
Am7(♭5)
gui-tars in card-board cas-es All night long.

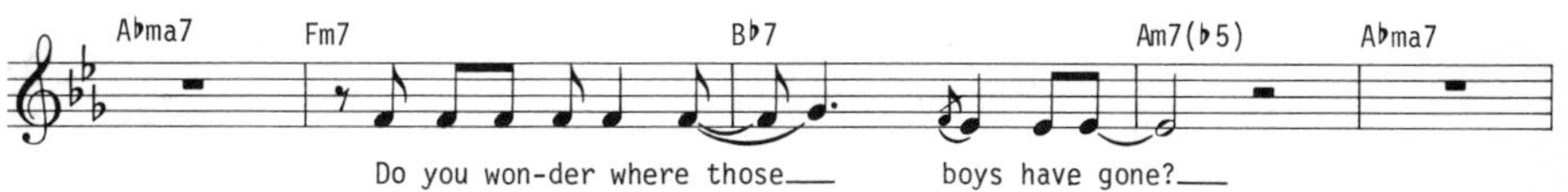
A♭ma7
Fm7
B♭7
Am7(♭5)
A♭ma7
Do you won-der where those boys have gone?

Fm7
B♭7
E♭𝄋
E♭𝄋
A♭𝄋
Do you won-der where those boys have gone?

A♭𝄋
E♭𝄋
A♭𝄋

food wrappers, empty bottles, full ashtrays. The song concludes with a shot of Jonah smoking a joint.

Early on a gloomy morning the van is again passing through an industrial landscape. Jonah is driving. John is in the front seat next to him working on a crossword puzzle. Danny and Lee-Andrew are in the middle seat talking. Clarence is looking out the window and making comments at any women who happen to walk by. Danny's monologue is intercut with John and Jonah's conversation about the club they will play next.

Danny . . . So the next day his manager calls me and says that Bob wants to do an album with me playing drums on it. I say, "What happened to his other drummer?" and the manager says, "Bob doesn't like him." Apparently they had like a falling out or something. So I says, "Sure, when are the dates?" and he says would I mind comin' down and sittin' in with the band just to make sure that everything locks in and sounds groovy and feels all right. I say, "I don't mind." So he told me to go to this rehearsal studio on West Fifty-second Street. I go down there and set up and there's nobody there. It's a fucking audition.

John What's this club like?

Jonah The Rising Sun? Well, when I first played it, it was a folk club on the circuit that everybody worked. Tom Paxton, Dave Van Ronk, New Lost City Ramblers, Bobby Gibson, Phil Ochs.

Danny So, check it out. It's me, the manager, and Bob the fucking superstar. Now the manager says can I play something.

Clarence The Rising Sun. It's pussy time. Get up. Boogety, boogety, boogety, boogety, shoop.

Jonah And then when everybody went electric, it became a blues club. J. Geils Band, Paul Butterfield Blues Band, Sonny Terry, Brownie McGhee. This was the first club I worked right after I married Marion. She used to travel with me then . . . nice times. . . . And then they changed owners and it became a rock club.

Jonah Seats about three hundred, three-fifty. Good sound system. Good audiences. You'll like it. You'll see. Don't eat the chili dog.

Danny So I say, "Play something? There's . . . what do you want me to play? There's no guitars, there's no keyboard, no bass. There's nobody here except me and those drums."

Jonah I can't believe I'm lost. I played this place a hundred times.

John Maybe we should stop and ask someone?

John Is that it? It says the Rising Sun.

Clarence I know where it is. You make a right here on Woodman. And I can still smell the scent in the air.

Danny So I play a shuffle. Now the manager says can I give it a little bit more foot. Bobby likes to push the bass drum on all his tracks. I said, "Well, I don't know. Let me ask. . . . Foot! What do you think, can you give us a little bit more?"

Clarence Hello, my dear. Clarence is here. The bigger the cushion, the better for pushin'.

The band pulls up in front of the Rising Sun. No sign of life. The marquee says THE ROCHES. *The club is deserted. A quick pan of the neighborhood and then a shot of the doors of the club nailed shut. A* FOR LEASE *sign is prominently posted.*

Danny It's closed.

Jonah I don't believe this. I don't believe this.

Danny Maybe you got the dates wrong.

Jonah (*Looks in his book*) No. I don't have the dates wrong. The twenty-fifth, twenty-sixth, twenty-seventh. The son of a bitch. He just confirmed with me three weeks ago. I don't believe this.

Danny You got his home number?

Jonah (*Checks his book again*) Five-nine-five one-nine-nine-one. Son of a bitch.

* * *

Jonah and the band are in a local bar and grill. Danny is playing pinball. Lee-Andrew and John are sitting in a booth. Clarence is standing at the bar, looking hostile. Jonah slides into the booth next to Lee-Andrew.

Jonah That was his wife. I'd like to kill the son of a bitch. He's gone. Left nine days ago. Took all the money from the joint account. Left her and the two kids.

Clarence What about our bread?

Jonah What *about* our bread?

Clarence Let me tell you somethin'. We been friends a long time, but I can't live off no four hundred dollars a week. That doesn't cover my alimony *or* my dope bills.

Danny (*Looking up from his game*) What dope bills? You haven't bought anything in years.

Clarence Fuck you, years.

Jonah You're not the only one with alimony and dope bills.

Clarence But I am the only one with enough brains to know when it's not workin'.

Jonah What did I do? Close that club just to fuck up Clarence Franklin?

John Hold it. We got enough money to get the plane tickets. Just calm down.

Lee-Andrew (*To Jonah, softly*) Ain't your fault the club closed, man.

Jonah Look, I'm sorry. What can I say? Bernie should have checked this out.

Clarence Check it out—yeah. Somebody shoulda checked it out. Well, I'm sorry too.

Jonah Hey, then, why don't you just quit? Don't threaten me. Just do it.

Clarence Maybe that's just what I'll do.

Jonah (*Looking down, talking almost to himself*) Then do it.

* * *

A shot of the street at night and the van pulling out. A heavy rain is falling. Shots of Jonah and the band through the windshield show everybody simply riding, nobody talking. Song "How the Heart Approaches What It Yearns" begins.

At the airport the arrival/departure board flashes: NEW YORK DELAYED. *A shot through the airport window shows a plane sitting outside in torrential rain. The camera moves to Jonah standing and looking out the window. The camera moves back to show people waiting in the airport waiting room and John talking to children, reading a book. Images of Jonah and Marion making love begin over the song and fade out to the following scene.*

* * *

In Marion's bedroom later that night, Jonah leans over and switches on the light. Marion and Jonah have the following conversation lying in bed.

Jonah Maybe I shouldn't be here when Matty wakes up.

Marion No. I think it's okay.

Jonah You haven't lost your magic touch.

Marion No. You haven't either.

Jonah I think post-separation agreement sex has got it all over premarital.

Marion Premarital wasn't bad. You threw in some new moves that I didn't remember. You must be getting a lot of practice.

Jonah No, I'm not.

Marion Yes, you are. You were always good at that stuff anyway.

Jonah So were you.

Marion So was I. You were good and I was good. Everything was always good.

Jonah Yes. That's the way it was.

Marion So how come it ended up in such a mess?

Jonah I don't know. Listen, let's get in a couple of more laughs here before we slip into our postcoital depression. Here's a joke for ya. There was a rabbi, a minister, and a . . .

Marion Jonah, look. I told you this wouldn't be good for me.

Jonah No, you didn't. You didn't say that.

Marion Well, I knew I was gonna have to pay for it later.

Jonah Yeah, but why does later have to come so soon?

Marion Oh, you mean why doesn't it come after you've gone so that *you* won't have to deal with it.

Jonah Hey, I was just . . . I was just trying to kid around.

Marion jumps out of bed and pulls on her bathrobe.

Marion No, Jonah, you can't come over here and sleep with me anytime you want and then go on your merry way.

Jonah I'm not on my merry way.

Marion And I'll tell you something. I'm sorry, but I don't care about the band anymore. What I care about . . .

Jonah (*Gets out of bed and starts dressing*) Oh, Christ.

Marion (*Sitting at her dressing table and shouting across the room*) Look, I don't care about the band breaking up. I care about our marriage breaking up. That you left Matty. And me. I don't know, Jonah. Look, if you love something, you have to *give*. You have to be there. Anyway, that's the way it is for me.

Awakened by the argument, Matty enters the bedroom wearing his pajamas. Sleepy, hands at his sides, he stands in the doorway.

Jonah Hey Matty. You okay? C'mere. (*Picks Matty up*) You okay?

Matty Yeah. Everybody's yelling so I woke up.

Marion I know, sweetheart. Come back to bed. I'll tuck you in.

Matty (*Hugs Jonah*) I want Daddy to tuck me in.

Jonah We'll both tuck you in.

Jonah carries Matty toward his bedroom. Marion goes with them. As they reach Matty's doorway:

Matty Is it too late for a story?

Jonah (*Putting Matty in bed*) It's after midnight.

Matty I stayed up until two o'clock once.

Jonah You did? Well, this is just not a good night for a story. You go to sleep now and I'll see you in the morning when the sun comes up.

Matty (*Looking directly at Jonah*) You're not *here* in the morning when the sun comes up.

Jonah You just go to sleep, okay?

Song "Oh, Marion" plays over the following scenes:

Jonah walks down a Greenwich Village street, stops at an open pizza stand and buys a slice, eats it standing and leaning against the counter.

Oh, Marion

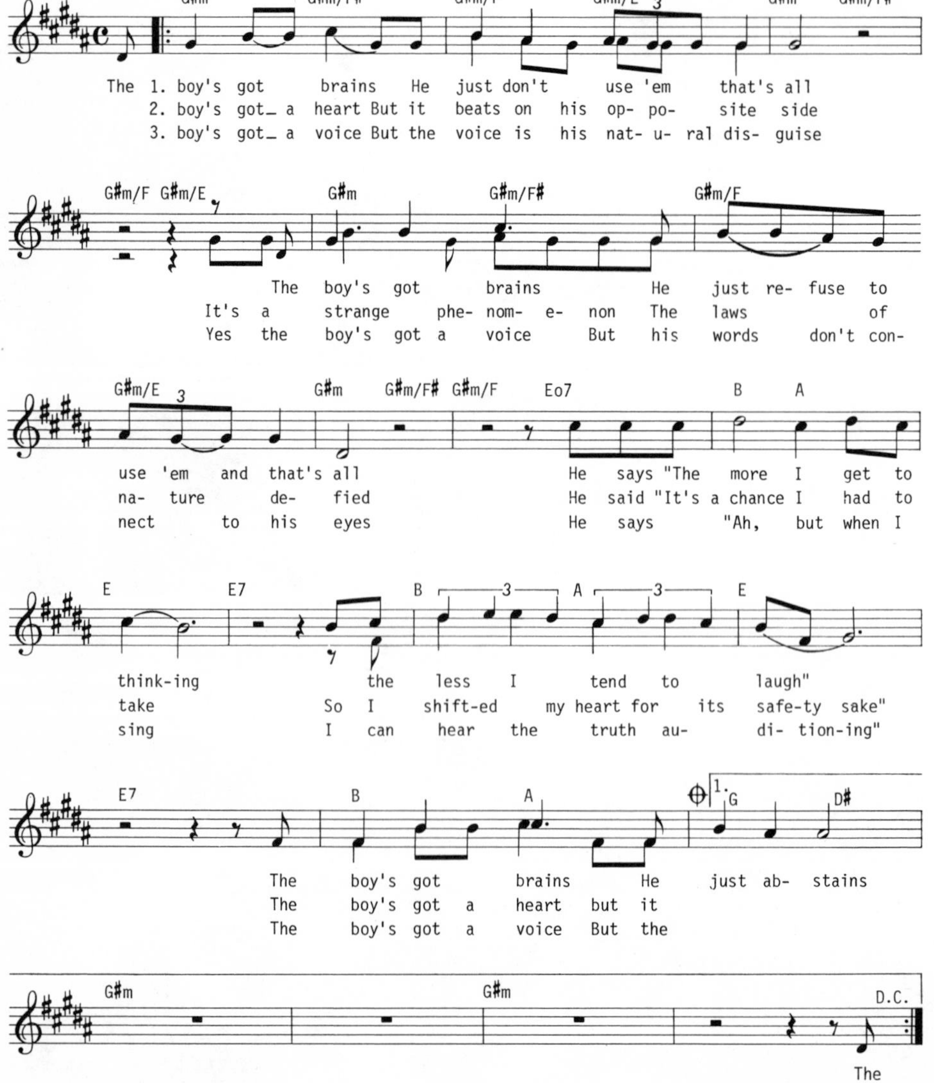
G#m
G#m/F#
G#m/F
G#m/E
The 1. boy's got brains He just don't use 'em that's all
2. boy's got_ a heart But it beats on his op- po- site side
3. boy's got_ a voice But the voice is his nat- u- ral dis- guise
The boy's got brains He just re- fuse to
It's a strange phe- nom- e- non The laws of
Yes the boy's got a voice But his words don't con-
Eo7
B
A
use 'em and that's all
na- ture de- fied
nect to his eyes
He says "The more I get to
He said "It's a chance I had to
He says "Ah, but when I
E
E7
think-ing the less I tend to laugh"
take So I shift-ed my heart for its safe-ty sake"
sing I can hear the truth au- di- tion-ing"
1. G
D#
The boy's got brains He just ab- stains
The boy's got a heart but it
The boy's got a voice But the
D.C.
The

2.
G
D#
Ab
beats on His op- po- site
Oh, Mar- i- on

Ab7/Gb
Fm7
Ao7
Bbm7
I think I'm in trou-ble here I should-'ve be- lieved you

Bbm7b5
Eb7
Ab
Abm7
When I heard you say-ing it The on- ly time That love is an

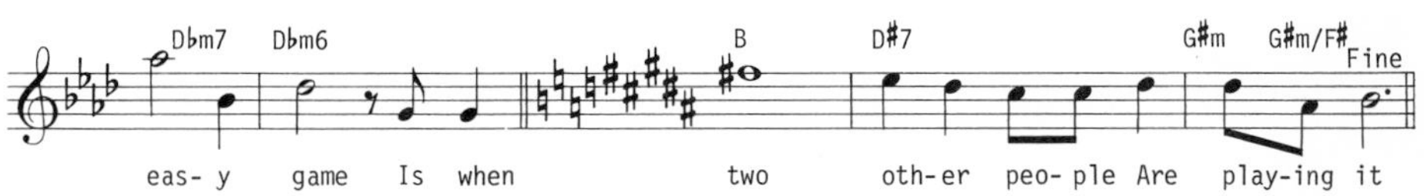
Dbm7
Dbm6
B
D#7
G#m
G#m/F#
Fine
eas- y game Is when two oth-er peo- ple Are play-ing it

G#m/F G#m/E G#m G#m/F# C#m/E D#7
D.C. al
G
D#
D.S. al Fine
Instrumental
The voice is his nat- u- ral

Jonah stands behind a stack of clothes, obviously his own, ready to be folded. Women surrounding him in the laundromat fold their clothes as he watches them out of the corner of his eye, folding his own clothes, mismatching socks.

Jonah walks down the street to a guitar store, buys some picks, asks the proprietor for strings.

Jonah walks down the street, turns the corner, and goes to his basement apartment.

As the song ends, Jonah is seen outside his apartment taking out the garbage.

* * *

Cut to an elevator. Jonah steps out into the reception room of the Premier Talent Agency. Gold records line all the walls. Jonah stops at the reception desk. The receptionist looks at her book and tells Jonah to go right in.

* * *

Inside Bernie Wepner's office, Bernie is seated, Jonah is pacing back and forth.

Bernie Okay, so there's a Radio and Records Convention in Chicago the last three days of the month. You're available. It's a big deal. Y'know, everybody in the business is gonna be there. Record people, radio people. They're gonna do a "Salute to the Sixties" night. They've got big acts. Sam and Dave. Lovin' Spoonful is gonna get back together for this. Tiny Tim. They're trying to get Dylan. They want you to do "Soft Parachutes." I think I can get you twenty-five hundred plus expenses.

Jonah Bernie, we don't even do that song anymore. I don't know if you realize this but the war has been over for several years.

Bernie Yeah, I heard. But a hit's always a hit, huh? Twenty-five hundred dollars. Who knows? Maybe the Beatles'll show.

Jonah Oh, definitely. I'm sure that as soon as the Beatles hear that the Jonah Levin Band is gonna do a . . .

Bernie . . . "Salute to the Sixties" night.

Jonah . . . "Salute to the Sixties" night . . . there's no question in my mind, they'll show.

Bernie Well, they don't want the band. They just want you.

Jonah Shit, I can't do that.

Bernie What are you talking about? The guys'll understand. They know the business. Look, Walter Fox is gonna be there, okay? Twenty-five hundred dollars. It's nostalgia. (*Softer*) Trust me.

* * *

Cut to Sam and Dave doing "Soul Man" onstage at the Drake Hotel. Jonah is backstage with the Lovin' Spoonful, enjoying the show, talking with John Sebastian, mugging with Sam and Dave's backup musicians from backstage. A shot of the audience shows Cal Van Damp with a beautiful woman at his side. Sam and Dave wind up their set.

In the hotel ballroom, the screen is in position for the slide show, which, along with a narration, provides for an intermission between acts.

Narrator While people listened and danced to the unique vibrance of folk-rock, to the Rolling Stones, Bob Dylan, and the Mamas and the Papas, the Rascals, it was possible to believe in magic. And a group from New York City captured that spark with an unmatched vitality . . . one of the best-loved bands of all time, the Lovin' Spoonful.

The stage manager comes backstage to lead the Spoonful onstage.

The Spoonful go onstage. The stage is in the form of a giant gold record, turning and lighted from below. A large neon sign says: "Radio and Records Chicago 1980." The band is to be spun into view of the audience, but they break into a run and shortcut the round revolving stage. As they perform their hit song "Do You Believe in Magic?" Jonah is still watching from backstage, getting a little drunk. Next he is in the dressing room talking to Tiny Tim, who is dressed in a comic-book cloth suit and is walking back and forth, practicing on his ukulele. Shots of Jonah backstage are intercut with shots of the audience, including Walter Fox with his wife, Lonnie, both looking impassive. As the Spoonful ends its performance, there is applause from both Jonah and the audience. The screen and narrator reappear to continue the slide show, which will lead to an introduction of Jonah.

Narrator The year is nineteen sixty-seven: *Sergeant Pepper,* perhaps the most important rock album of all time, is released and instantly recognized as a landmark achievement.

Jonah is backstage watching the slide show as Tiny Tim paces back and forth, strumming his uke and practicing.

Jonah Are those the changes to the song you were playing in the dressing room?

Tiny Tim nods curtly and continues to pace.

Narrator A shift was taking place in America. The life style of youth

became more and more emphatically opposed to the once sacred standards of their parents.

This era would launch the record business to new heights of unprecedented growth and success, overtaking motion pictures as the most popular medium in the entertainment industry, with sales of over two billion dollars.

The stage manager comes backstage to escort Jonah to the stage. Jonah is pacing with his guitar. Dave is watching the slide show. Sam enters from a dressing room.

Jonah Real nice.

Sam Thank you.

Narrator Along with Bob Dylan and Joan Baez, no performer more thoroughly expressed the emotional temperament of the age than Jonah Levin, whose brilliant anthem "Soft Parachutes" stands as an enduring monument of this period.

The stage goes black. Jonah steps onto the darkened disc. As the light comes on, the disc revolves him toward the audience and applause. Jonah steps off the record and moves to the mike to sing "Soft Parachutes." At the conclusion of the song, there is first a pause, then some nervous applause.

* * *

Cut to Walter Fox's party after the concert. The suite is packed with the rich and famous of the record industry. Jonah leans against the stairwell. A waiter passes by with several glasses of champagne on a tray. A good-looking girl descends the staircase and Jonah vaguely follows her. However, when he sees her approach Cal Van Damp, he tries vainly to step away.

Cal (*To girl*) Houston. Hi, gorgeous. What took you so long? (*To Jonah*) Hey, Albert Schweitzer, what's the good word? Nice set you did tonight. Very music and spectacle.

Jonah Hey, Cal Van Damp, what's the good word with you?

Cal I don't know. You're the bright boy. I figured you'd know.

Jonah Steatopygous.

Radio and Records

Radio and Records Chicago 1980

NY

Cal What?

Jonah It means a large rump. A fat ass.

Cal's date giggles. Cal senses embarrassment heading his way.

Cal Really? Why is that the good word?

Jonah Because, like, let's say I was to say, "Cal, you have a fat ass," you might be offended. But if I say, "Cal, you're looking steatopygous," you wouldn't know what the fuck I was talking about. Do ya?

Cal I hope you don't have any plans for getting your records played on the radio in the near future.

Jonah (*Insolently casual*) Not really, no.

Jonah walks away.

Cal Good. Because you won't get any. Nice talking to you, Schweitzer. (*To girl*) Real little prick. Don't you think?

Girl (*Stupidly*) I couldn't tell.

Cal approaches Walter. Cal is muttering, still angry and pointing across the room to Jonah. Over the noise and music of the party he is heard threatening to leave if Jonah stays. Walter promises to take care of Jonah and approaches Lonnie, who is chatting comfortably with John Sebastian. They both are leaning on the piano. Walter excuses himself and tells Lonnie to get Jonah out, explaining briefly about Cal Van Damp. Jonah has gone to the bar for another glass of wine and is standing there alone as Lonnie approaches him. She is a little tipsy herself. Lonnie gives Jonah a long look, leans on the bar beside him, and begins speaking slowly and distinctly.

Lonnie Hello.

Jonah Hello.

Lonnie Remember me?

Jonah I sure do. You're . . .

Lonnie Walter . . . Walter has asked me to discreetly get you out of here before you do any more harm to him or yourself. He mumbled something about Cal Van Damp's ass. Did you say something about that?

Jonah I did. I mentioned that it was fat. It's fat.

Lonnie Ah. Veracity aside for the moment, Walter feels that your presence here could be disruptive and he has asked me to entice you to leave.

Jonah (*Pointing*) That's Dick . . . of Dick and Dede. . . . Entice me to leave?

Lonnie Actually, he just said, "Get him out." I added the enticement part. It seemed a much more appealing exit line.

Jonah I bet Dede's here. I think they're getting back together again. . . . What enticements did he have in mind?

Lonnie He had none.

Jonah What enticements did you have in mind?

Lonnie Take my hand.

Jonah and Lonnie walk down the long hallway toward the elevators. Approaching them is a night chambermaid.

Lonnie Excuse me. I left my key in my room. Would you be so kind as to open it for me?

Chambermaid What room are you in, ma'am?

Lonnie Right here. Forty-four forty-two. . . . Thank you so much.

Lonnie steps inside the room and flicks on the light.

Jonah (*Putting his arms around Lonnie*) How come you have this room when you have the big suite upstairs?

Lonnie I don't. I just thought we might make some use of it while the occupants are out.

Jonah Where are they, at the party?

That's Why God Made the Movies

E E/D# E9/D C#7 F#7 F#7/G# F#/A F#/A#
stole a- way in-to the night Hop-ing things would work out right
B E7 F#m7 E7/G#
That's why God made the mov- ies Say you will, say you
A E/G# F#m7 E
will Say you'll take me to your lov- ing breast
E F#m7
Say you'll nour- ish me with your ten- der- ness
B7sus C#m B E F#m7 E7/G#
The way the la-dies some- times do Say you won't, say
A E/G# F#m7 Ema7
you won't Say you won't leave me for no oth-er man
Ema7 F#m7 B/D#
Say you'll love me just the way I am Say you'll love me
B E7 A7 E7
Say you will, say you will
A7 E7 A7 E7 A7
E7 A7 E7 A7
𝄋 al ⊕
When I was born
⊕ B
That's why God That's why God That's why God made the
E7 A7
mov-ies

Lonnie I have no idea, really.

Jonah and Lonnie walk toward the bed together.

Jonah You mean they could come in at any moment?

Lonnie (*Looking at her watch*) It's unlikely but it's possible.

Jonah (*Surprised and amused*) You're crazy.

Lonnie (*Looking at Jonah mock-seriously*) That's part of the enticement.

Jonah and Lonnie sit on the end of the bed, holding hands and looking at each other provocatively.

* * *

Jonah and Matty leave Marion's apartment building. They are mock-boxing as they round the corner.

The Song "That's Why God Made Movies" plays over the following scenes:

Jonah and Matty are in Playland, an electronic game and pinball place, playing an intense game of air hockey. They go into a recording booth and together record a song.

Jonah and Matty walk out of a movie theater which is showing The Empire Strikes Back. *They are deep in discussion about the movie. Their faces are reflected on the glass case that contains stills from the movie.*

Jonah and Matty walk around the Village, past roller skaters and people playing in the streets.

The song ends as they enter Jonah's basement apartment.

* * *

Matty and Jonah are seen in the bathroom mirror. Both have shaving cream smeared over their faces and both are shaving, Jonah with a real razor and Matty with a red and yellow plastic razor.

Matty Hey, Dad.

Jonah Mm-hmm.

Matty Maybe if I'm gonna be sleeping over at your house . . . maybe I'll bring some of my toys.

Jonah Yeah, that would be a good idea. Which toys would you bring?

Matty Oh, maybe my parcheesi set . . . or my trains . . .

Jonah Mm-hmm.

Matty . . . and some other stuff.

Jonah (*Examining Matty's face*) Missed a spot right over here.

Matty Oh, I see.

Jonah Be very careful. That's very sharp, you know.

Matty Oh, okay.

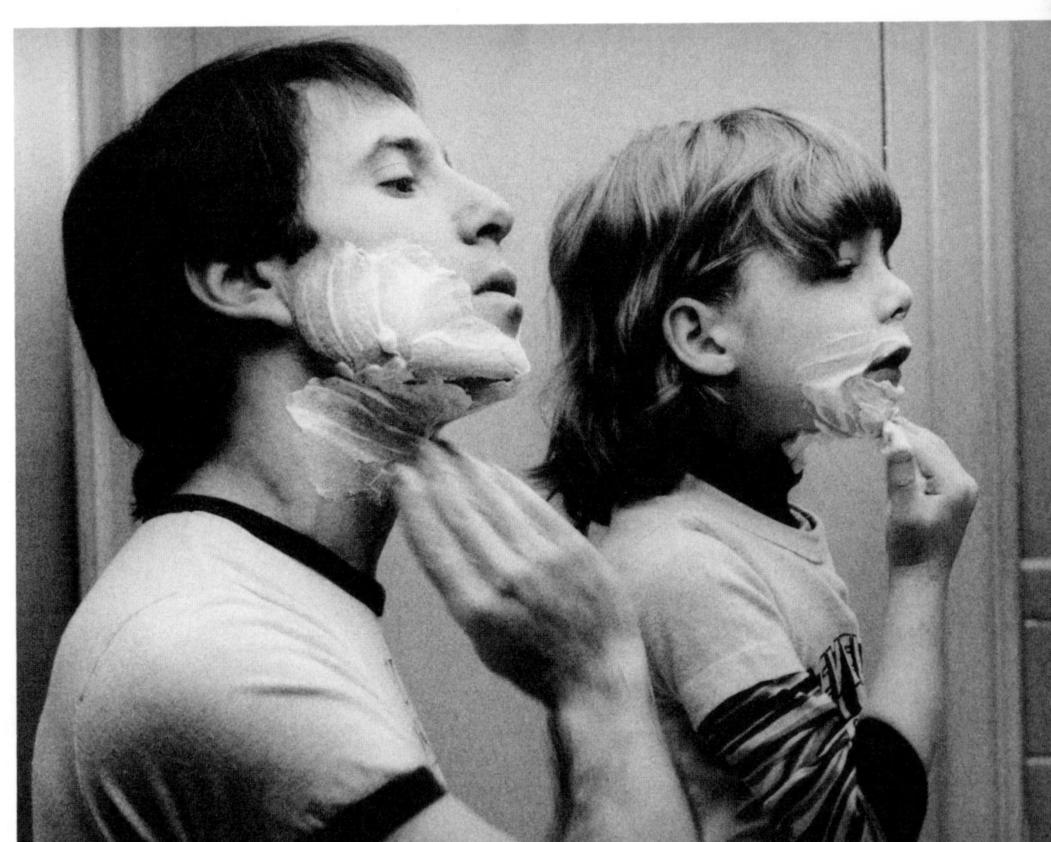

Jonah Yeah, get under there (*watching Matty*). Don't shave directly across your lips. (*More shaving*) Good. Very good. You're an excellent shaver, I must say.

Matty Thanks, Dad.

Jonah Don't mention it, son.

Jonah hugs Matty and both of them burst out laughing.

* * *

In Walter Fox's office building, Jonah is walking down the hallway lined with gold records. He passes the "Soft Parachutes" record and continues on. He is ushered into Walter's suite of offices and walks past several oversize super-realistic paintings to a large round table where Walter sits drinking coffee. Walter has obviously just finished lunch and is still being served by a waiter. Walter stands up to shake Jonah's hand.

Walter Sit down, my friend.

Jonah How are you?

Walter Would you like some coffee?

Jonah Yeah, I'd love some.

Walter Had quite a time in Chicago, didn't you? My wife found your comments to Cal Van Damp very amusing.

Jonah Well, I owe you an apology for . . .

Walter No. Actually, it was quite funny. What was that word?

Jonah Steatopygous.

Walter Steatopygous. I'll have to remember to use that somewhere. . . . Those new songs of yours—I was distracted when I first heard them, but I agree with my wife. They're very impressive, something there. . . .

Jonah Thank you.

Walter (*Dialing his secretary but talking to Jonah*) I'm going to call in Steve Kunelian. He's a young producer that I think someday will be very important. (*To secretary*) Kathy, call in Steve for a minute, will you, please? (*To Jonah*) You'll like him, I think he has a good sense of the Top Forty. A good sense of what's danceable too. He's very Top Forty–oriented. That's the kind of album you should cut. Don't you agree?

Jonah (*Surprised at the turn of events*) Yeah . . . Yeah . . .

Steve Kunelian enters. He is a thin, dark man in his mid-thirties with short, perfectly barbered hair. He is dressed in jeans. The waiter leaves.

Walter Steve, this is Jonah Levin.

Jonah rises from his chair.

Jonah Hi. We've met before.

Steve (*Shakes Jonah's hand but looks intensely at Walter*) I remember.

Walter I'd like you two to collaborate. Keep your eyes out for singles possibilities. Something that has integrity . . . but is still commercial.

Steve When do you want me to start?

Walter Anytime. Next week. . . . Is that good for you, Jonah?

Jonah Yeah. That's fine. It'll give me a chance to rehearse some with my band.

Steve Oh . . . your band . . . I have an idea about that.

Walter (*To Steve*) Well, now's the time to discuss it.

Steve I've been working with a rhythm section that I really think is good. I'd like to use them.

Walter Jonah, is that a problem for you? If you use Steve's rhythm section?

Jonah Yeah. That's a problem for me. I always work with my band.

Steve You worked without them in Chicago.

Jonah That was a big mistake. I shouldn't have done that. I can't do that again. I've worked with these guys for ten years now.

Steve Could we do an experimental session?

Jonah Not without the band. I can't do that.

Walter Boys, let's don't make a melodrama out of this. Steve, why don't you work with Jonah's . . . ?

The phone rings. Walter picks it up.

Walter I'll be with them in a minute. . . . I'm afraid I'm going to have to

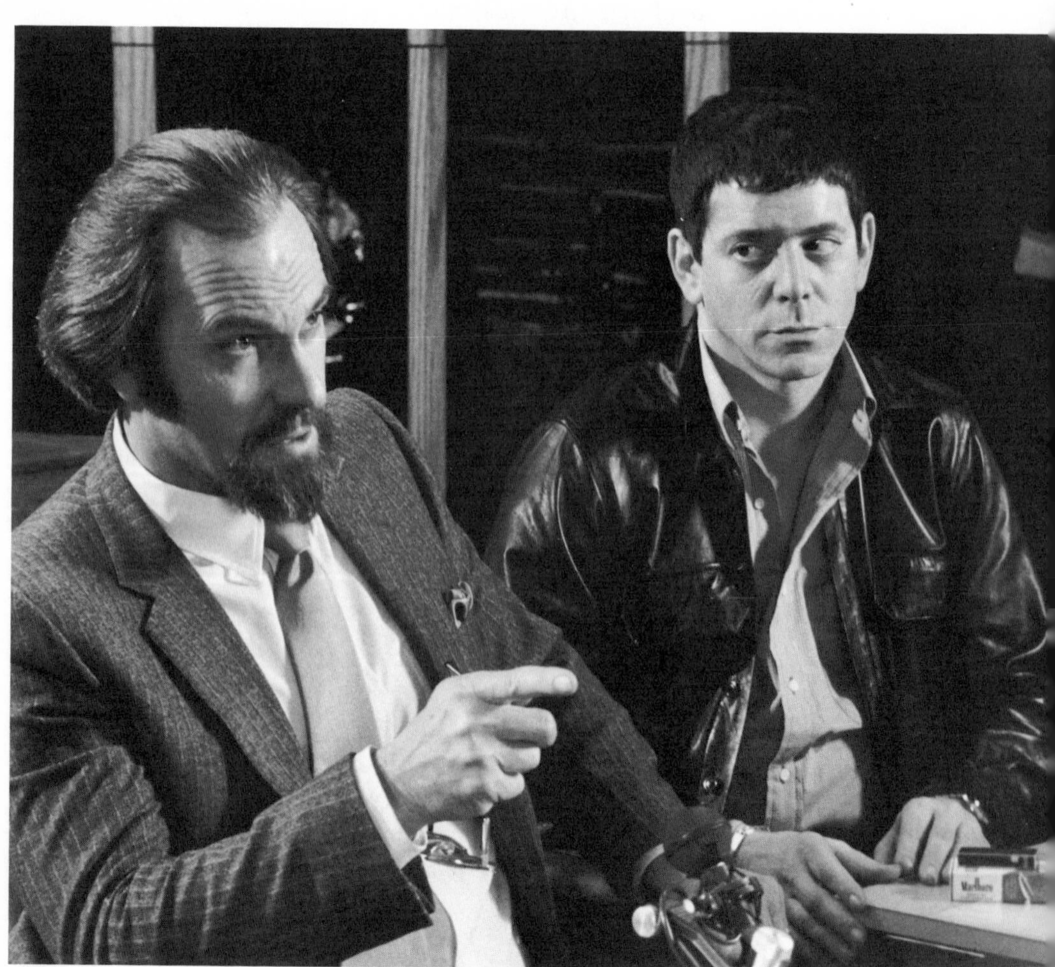

kick you guys out of here. I have some people waiting but it seems like we have a plan of action here. Steve?

Steve Absolutely.

Walter All right, my friend?

Jonah Yeah. Yeah. (*To Steve*) Nice to see you again.

Steve Nice to see you.

Steve leaves. Walter and Jonah start to the door.

Walter Are you happy?

Jonah I really appreciate this. Listen, I never figured that you'd ever want to see me again or talk to me . . .

Walter Jonah.

Jonah pauses at the door. Walter closes the door.

Walter You wouldn't by chance be fucking my wife?

Jonah, taken by surprise, is silent.

Walter Because that wouldn't be conducive to a good artist-record company relationship.

* * *

Cut to Lonnie Fox's bedroom, overlooking Central Park on Fifth Avenue. It is a large, bright, airy room done entirely in neutral shades: beige carpet, beige walls, a large bed with satin sheets. Jonah and Lonnie are in bed together.

Jonah What was I gonna say? Yes, Walter, I am sort of fucking your wife.

Lonnie Is that what we're doing? Sort of fucking?

Jonah rises and sits on the windowsill. Behind him is Central Park in panorama.

Jonah Well, what are we doing? Why do I come here? Why did you call me?

Lonnie You're here because you came. I called you because you needed a job and I was sympathetic.

Jonah Is this my job?

Lonnie climbs out of bed, wrapping herself in a white satin robe. She goes to the closet and begins putting on white silk pants and blouse. During the following conversation Jonah paces around the room as Lonnie dresses very slowly.

Lonnie I don't hire my lovers. I can still score my points on the honor system. No, I'm not the one who's desperate.

Jonah I don't want to make my record because you told Walter to give me a break.

Lonnie You've got that all wrong. You should learn to take a friend's help when it's offered.

Jonah Did you tell Walter to let me record?

Lonnie No.

Jonah It was entirely his idea?

Lonnie pauses to consider her next answer.

Lonnie No.

Jonah is silent. He is again sitting on the windowsill, where Lonnie joins him.

Lonnie I'll be forty-five years old on my next birthday, the exact date of which I have succeeded in erasing from my memory. I don't particularly like the record business. I don't enjoy the conventions. I don't like going backstage. I don't smoke dope. I gave it up when they were still calling it reefers. I lost interest ten years ago. You, on the other hand . . . you want this record. You need it. I'd like to see you get it. Take a friend's help when it's offered.

* * *

Jonah is in the recording studio, wearing headphones, playing his electric guitar. The camera pulls back to show Steve Kunelian in the control booth with two engineers, Jonah in the

recording studio with his band, working on "Ace in the Hole." Steve directs the session from the control booth. His initial comments to the engineers are heard over the band as they rehearse.

Steve Okay, Bob. It doesn't seem to be sitting just quite right with the track. I'd like to bring the rhythm section up a little bit. Maybe you can hear it better. Play a little more into it, okay? Great.

Jonah (*Singing*)
. . . where you been so long
Don't you know me
I'm your ace in the hole . . .

Steve Make the bass a little less tubby and bring the drum up. . . . Jesus, you know, guitar's a little bluesy. He's really good, but he's so bluesy.

Jonah Ace in the hole
Lean on me
Don't you know me
I'm your guarantee . . .

Steve Take the piano out—hold it—take out the vocal. . . . Bring the piano up. Can I have more of the piano?

Jonah Riding on this rolling bus . . .

Steve Listen to this. (*The piano can be heard.*) If you listen carefully, he's doin' those kind of licks that should be somethin' else maybe. Maybe a sax or something.

Jonah And the smokestacks drifting by . . .

Steve Kind of open it up. Could you do something about the snare? Make it a little fatter?

Jonah In the hour when the heart is weakest . . .

Steve There it is. Doesn't that remind you of strings? That would be pretty—strings. That would be nice. . . . Get the vocal out.

Jonah When time has stopped
But the bus just rolls along . . .

Steve It's always the same style as before. All right. Hit that talk-back. (*To Jonah*) Okay, that's really terrific. . . . Wait, hold it a minute. (*To engineer*) Take it off. Take it off.

The engineer takes the talk button off. Steve turns to him.

Steve What's the drummer's name?

Engineer Danny.

Steve talks to the members of the band through the control booth microphone. The band listens, nodding in response.

Steve (*Indicates that he wants the talk button back on*) Danny, you wanna give me a little more foot on that? It's a little lame. And also on the cymbal, when it's ch-ch-ch-ch-ch, on the accent, on the "and," a little push. . . . Clarence, you're great. . . . Jonah, you're great. . . . Lee-Andrew, let's . . . uhh . . . do your licks as an overdub. I think it'll work out a lot better. . . . Jonah, I think it's terrific. I think we should go for one. I just wish you'd hold your voice back a little bit. I'm a little worried. Y'know, let's just use your voice for a guide vocal and not blow it. Other than that, I think we got it. Why don't we go for one? Okay? Ready? Great.

Cut to Jonah and Clarence in the studio, sometime later, laying down the vocal onto the finished track.

Jonah and Clarence Some people say music is the ace in the hole
Just your ordinary rhythm and blues
Your basic rock and roll
You can sit on the top of the beat
You can lean on the side of the beat
You can hang from the bottom of the beat
But you gotta admit that the music is sweet

Hey, Junior, I'm your ace in the hole
(I'm callin' you)
Hey, Junior, I'm your ace in the hole
(I'm talkin' to you)
Hey, Junior, I'm your ace in the hole
(I'm callin' you)
Hey, Junior, I'm your ace in the hole

Steve, in the control booth, watching and listening, turns to the engineer to hit the talk-back.

Steve That's great. I really liked that. Why don't you come in and you can hear it back. And, Jonah, I want to talk to you, okay? I have some ideas I'd like to talk to you about.

Jonah and Clarence take off their headphones and head for the booth.

In the control booth Steve, Jonah, and Clarence listen to the playback. As it ends:

Steve Anyway, let me continue. Electric piano that Clarence is playing on the bridge. There's a beautiful thing that I think we can have some strings in there. A nice string section . . . ahh, c'mon, it'd tear your heart out.

Jonah Yeah, well, it's not that we don't want our hearts torn out, it's just that we want to make a ballsy record and not a lush . . .

Steve I want to make a ballsy record too. "River Deep, Mountain High"—now that's a ballsy record, wouldn't you say? Strings in there. So we open it up texturally, then maybe we could add . . . saxophone, on the end . . . in the solo . . . on the "Roll on, roll on" part. A nice tough sax.

Jonah You mean replace Lee-Andrew's guitar solo?

Steve Absolutely . . . right.

Jonah Oh, I can't. I can't do that to Lee-Andrew. He's the lead guitar player.

Steve Sure he is, sure he is. This doesn't take away from Lee-Andrew. I'm sure he'd love it too. Just broaden things a little bit. Y'know? Don't you want to try for some AM air play on this?

Jonah Well, you tell him. I'm not gonna go to Lee-Andrew and tell him that his solo is out.

Steve I'm not asking you to, man. Let him listen to it. Let everybody listen to it. I'm sure you'll love it. I'm sure he'll love it.

Jonah What makes you so sure? You don't know.

Steve Hey, listen, y'know. What do you think I am? Just a knob-turner here? I made some—I made a couple of records myself, y'know. I know what I'm doin'. I'm not here just to play with you. I know what I'm doing. Why don't you just listen?

* * *

In the recording studio, Steve is overdubbing a saxophone solo. Next he overdubs a large string section. It is a lush and cliché-ridden arrangement. Then there is a percussionist playing congas and cowbell. Finally, a group of girl singers overdub the "Roll on, roll on" section. Inside the control booth all of this is added to Jonah's track.

* * *

Later, Jonah, the band, Steve, and Walter Fox are listening intently to a playback of Steve's finished track. The song is ruined. Jonah leans against the console. Steve and Walter are sitting with the engineer behind the board. The band is variously placed around the room. The playback ends.

Walter Very exciting. Very. Well, I certainly think we've accomplished what we set out to do.

Steve I think so.

Walter Absolutely. I want to hear it again, but I must say, on first listening, it's very . . . powerful. Are you happy, Jonah?

ace in the Hole

A7 Bm7/F# A7/G A7 Bm7/F# A7/G
Some peo- ple say Je- sus that's the ace in the hole
Two hun-dred dol- lars, that's my ace in the hole When I'm
Once I was cra- zy and my ace in the hole Was that I
Some peo- ple say mu- sic that's their ace in the hole Just your
A7 Bm7 A7/G A7 Bm7/F# A7/G
But I nev- er met the man so I don't real- ly know
down, dirt- y and des-per-ate That's my e- merg-en- cy bank roll I got
knew that I was cra-zy So I nev- er lost my self-con-trol I just
ord-i-nar- y rhythm and blues Your bas- ic rock and roll You can
A7 Bm7/(F#) A7/G A7 Bm7/F# A7/G
May- be some Christ-mas if I'm sick and a- lone He will
Two hun-dred dol- lars, that's the price on the street If you
walk in the mid-dle of the road I sleep in the mid-dle of the bed I
sit on the top of the beat You can lean on the side of the beat You can
A7 Bm7/(F#) A7/G A7
look up my num-ber Call me on the phone and say
wan- na get some qual- i- ty That's the price you got to meet and the man says
stop in the mid-dle of a sen-tence And the voice in the mid-dle of my head said
hang from the bot-tom of the beat But you got to ad-mit that the mu-sic is sweet
G/D Bm7 F#m7
1. Hey, boy, where you been so long
2. Hey, Jun- ior,
3. Hey, Jun- ior,
4. (tacet)
G#m7/(♭5) 1.2. Dm/F A7 Bm7/F# A7/G
Don't you know me I'm your ace in the hole
A7 Bm7/F# A7/G 3.4. Dm/F
I'm your ace in the hole

A/E
Eb7(b4-b5)
Dma7
C#07
A#07
Oh yeah Ace in the hole Lean on me
Bm7
4th x
Dm6
E9
A
Bm/A
A7
Don't you know me I'm your guar-an- tee
Drums
Same Tempo (Shuffle Feel)
G/D
G
Rid-ing on this roll- ing bus
F#m7
F#m7
Bm7
Be- neath a ston- y sky With a slow moon ris- ing
E7
A
A7
And the smoke- stacks drift-ing by
G/D
G
F#m7
In the hour when the heart is weak-est And the mem-o- ry is strong
Bm7
E
When time has stopped But the bus just rolls a-long
A
Drum
18
D.C. to 4th verse and Coda
Dm/F
E7sus
A7 A7/F# Bm7/G A/G#
A7 A7/F# Bm7/G A/G#
I'm your guar-an- tee
A7
Bm7/F# A7/G
Instrumental vamp followed by words of 4th verse
(8 bars only)

Jonah I like a lot of it, but Steve said anything we didn't like, we could change. Y'know, like some of the overdubs.

Walter It's the most commercial thing you've cut in a long time.

Clarence You really think so.

Walter I know so. But I want to listen again and I want to hear what you've got to say. Steve, you really did a fine job. All of you. Really, you should all be very pleased. Let's hear it.

Jonah and the band are talking outside the studio.

Clarence Is this the way it's gonna be on the record?

Jonah Hey, we don't have to take it. We'll just tell Walter we don't like it.

Clarence You tell him. It's your song. It's your band. You tell him.

Jonah walks quickly back into the control booth.

Danny (*Calling after him*) Tell him I loved the percussion.

Walter, Steve, and the engineer are in the control booth. Walter has his coat on and is speaking on the phone. Jonah enters. There is a confrontation in mime which the camera witnesses through the studio window. Finally, Walter pats Jonah on the back and exits, leaving Jonah alone with Steve.

* * *

Jonah is standing outside Marion's apartment. She opens the door.

Marion What's up?

Jonah Can I come in?

Marion Sure. Come on in. Were you recording tonight?

Jonah Yeah. I was in the studio. (*Peeking toward the living room*) Am I interrupting, uh . . . ?

Marion Well, I was watching *Mrs. Miniver* . . . Greer Garson . . .

Jonah A classic. My boy's asleep?

Marion Mm-hmm. After a bitter battle over whether he should be allowed to stay up and watch "Love Boat," or not.

Jonah Who won?

Marion Who do you think?

Jonah Did he beat you with logic or with tears?

Marion A combo, actually. Wait, I want to show you something.

Marion steps into the bedroom and returns with a piece of paper.

Marion Matty's been working on a song.

Marion hands the piece of paper to Jonah.

Jonah (*Reading*)
"Hey, baby, don't be cruel
I'm gonna pick you up
And we'll have a date
At the pizza parlor
You can have a pizza and
I can have one too
But she didn't want a pizza
So I said
So long, babe."

See that? And you were worried that he was gonna be a songwriter.

Marion Who knew we had a borderline genius?

Jonah Maybe a little too much emphasis on the pizza. You got any Percodan?

Marion No. But I've got some aspirin in the bathroom. What's wrong?

Jonah Pain. Just pain.

Jonah and Marion walk through the hall to the bathroom.

Marion You really should watch it, you know. You just like to take pills.

Jonah Who, me? Well, that's the truth.

Marion You sound like Matty.

Jonah I am Matty. Just older.

Marion Here's your aspirin.

Jonah That's not what I really need.

Marion What do you need?

Jonah A job.

Marion A job?

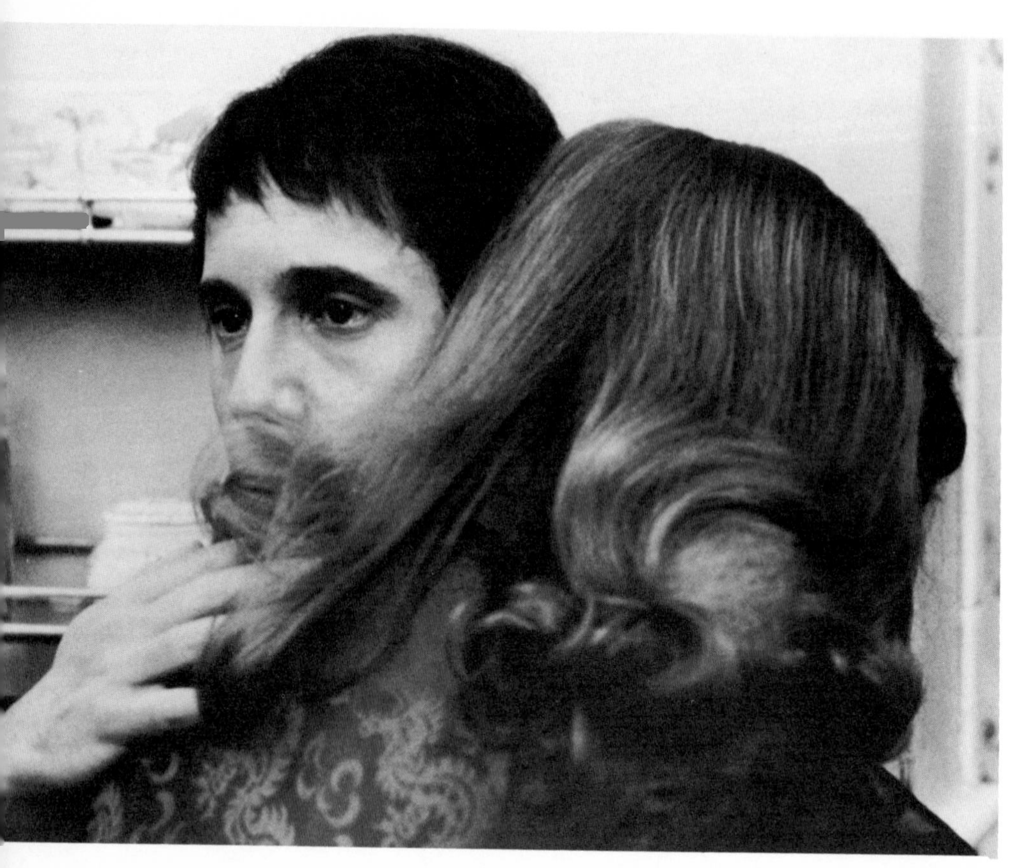

Jonah A hug?

Marion Jonah, what are you talking about?

Jonah I figure the band has broken up.

Marion But that's crazy. What about the album?

Jonah Gone.

Marion I don't understand. I thought you said everything was going well.

They embrace. Tears come to Jonah's eyes.

Marion You said everything was going well.

Jonah Remember the time that we were doing it on the kitchen table and the baby-sitter walked in?

Marion Yes, I remember that. You jumped off and hid behind the refrigerator. I had to sit there with my pants down trying to act composed.

Jonah She looked like a panicky rabbit.

Marion *She* did? I was the one that was sitting there bare-assed. And you were the coward.

Jonah We had some good times, didn't we?

Marion Yeah, lots. Jonah, what happened tonight?

Jonah (*Imitating in a southern accent the talking part of an early Elvis Presley record*)
"Honey, you lied when you said
You loved me
And I was a fool to care
But I'd rather go on
Believing your lies
Than living without you
(*Singing*)
"Are you lonesome tonight
Are you lonesome tonight"

Jonah, with his arms around Marion, leads her toward the bedroom.

* * *

Cut to Jonah sitting alone at a bar drinking a beer. The song "Jonah" is playing as the camera follows Jonah outside and down the street. Jonah is carrying his guitar case and walking fast.

* * *

Jonah enters the recording studio building. A receptionist is polishing her nails at the front desk.

Jonah I think I left my glasses in the studio this afternoon.

Receptionist *(Motions him past)* Okay.

Jonah Thanks.

Jonah exits toward the control booth. He enters the empty control booth and switches on the light. He finds the shelf where the tapes are stored. One of the boxes says: "Master—Jonah Levin." Jonah opens his guitar case, which is empty, and places the master tape in the case. He takes a pair of glasses from his pocket and puts them on. He exits with the tape inside the case.

* * *

Out on the West Side Manhattan street, Jonah stops and opens his guitar case. He removes the tape and, holding on to one end, hurls the reel down the middle of the street so that the tape unwinds in the gutter. The tape flaps in the wind down the length of the empty street.

Movie ends with a verse of "One-Trick Pony."

a Note on the Type

The text of this book was set in a film version of Melior, a typeface designed by Hermann Zapf and issued in 1952. Born in Nuremberg, Germany, in 1918, Zapf has been a strong influence in printing since 1939. Melior, like Times Roman, another popular twentieth-century typeface, was created specifically for use in a newspaper. With this functional end in mind, Zapf nonetheless chose to base the proportions of its letterforms on those of the golden section. The result is a typeface of unusual strength and surpassing subtlety.

Composition by American-Stratford Graphic Services, Inc., Brattleboro, Vermont. Printing and Binding by Halliday Lithograph, West Hanover, Massachusetts.

Book design by Albert Chiang.